THE DAILY READING BIBLE

Volume 19

TITUS   ISAIAH 13-27   TEN COMMANDMENTS

The Daily Reading Bible (Volume 19)
© Matthias Media 2009

Matthias Media
(St Matthias Press Ltd ACN 067 558 365)
PO Box 225
Kingsford NSW 2032
Australia
Ph: (02) 9663 1478; Int. +61-2-9663-1478
Fax: (02) 9663 3265; Int. +61-2-9663-3265
Email: info@matthiasmedia.com.au
Internet: www.matthiasmedia.com.au

Matthias Media (USA)
Ph: 724 964 8152; Int. +1-724-964-8152
Fax: 724 964 8166; Int. +1-724-964-8166
Email: sales@matthiasmedia.com
Internet: www.matthiasmedia.com

ISBN 978 1 921441 41 7

Cover design and typesetting by Matthias Media.
Series concept design by www.madebydesign.com.au

CONTENTS

INTRODUCTION

Reading our Bibles regularly is getting **harder.** That, at least, seems to be the common experience of many Christians. We could waste lots of ink speculating on the reasons for this: is it the frenetic pace of life these days? Is it spiritual laziness? Is it the impact of postmodernism on our culture and the lack of certainty when it comes to interpreting the written word?

But a better option than speculating on the reasons, we thought, was to provide a new resource for Christians to help them get back into a more regular habit of reflecting daily on God's word. So back in June 2001, we decided to start including a section called 'Bible Brief' in our monthly magazine, *The Briefing* (see www.matthiasmedia.com.au for more information about *The Briefing*). The 'Bible Brief' provided 20 short readings each month—acknowledging that there will be days we miss or days when we want to do something a bit different—with questions, thoughts to ponder, and suggestions to get started in prayer.

Now, several years later, we have a good collection of 'Bible Briefs', and it's time to offer them to a wider audience in a format that will, we hope, be even more convenient and useful.

This nineteenth volume contains 60 readings, all designed to be done in 15–20 minutes. These daily Bible readings are designed to help you feed regularly from God's word. They won't cover every issue in each passage, nor even every passage from each Bible book. In other words, *they are no substitute for the in-depth study of the Scriptures* that you may undertake personally, in small groups or through listening to sermons.

With the kind permission of our friends at Crossway Bibles, we've been able to make this a complete package to take with you—we've included the English Standard Version Bible text with each daily study. So you can take this one book with you and have everything you need—on the train, on the bus, or to the park at lunchtime—wherever and whenever you can get 20 minutes to yourself.

How to use these readings
- *With a penitent heart*, the true prerequisite for all Bible reading. Open with prayer (perhaps using the prayer suggested at the beginning of each set of studies).
- *With 15–20 minutes* of peace and quiet. If you can take longer, and want to read and pray further—great! But we have designed the readings to be done in a fairly short space of time.
- *With an accurate modern translation.* We recommend and have included the new ESV translation. The writers of the studies refer to this translation. Contact us for further details about the ESV or visit www.matthiasmedia.com.au/ESV

- *With a pen.* Even if you only jot down brief ideas, writing focuses the mind.
- *As a guide and help, not a straitjacket.* Feel free to dig further into the passage, to notice and ponder things that the questions don't point to.
- *As a launch-pad for prayer.* Use the prayer ideas at the end of each reading as a starting point for your daily prayer. Many of the points that will arise from the readings will be things you can pray for yourself, and also for others (family, friends, neighbours, etc.). Why not compile a list of people you want to pray for (you can write them in the blank space below), and use the prayer ideas from each reading to pray for the next person on your list?

This nineteenth volume includes:
- studies on Titus (written by Ross Blunden and Andrew Prince, pastors at Bayside Baptist Church in Brisbane, Australia)
- studies on Isaiah 13-27 (written by Tony Wright, assistant minister at St Alban's Anglican Church in Lindfield, Sydney, Australia)
- studies on the Ten Commandments (written by Al Stewart who is a full-time ministry worker in the Wollongong region, Australia, and Simon Roberts, associate minister at St George North Anglican Church in Sydney, Australia).

Matthias Media
July 2009

Please note: the main section of Scripture for each study is reproduced before the questions. Other Scripture references are reproduced as footnotes at the bottom of the page, or, where the passages are too long to be included as footnotes, in the appendix.

PEOPLE TO PRAY FOR:

TITUS

INTRODUCTION

Titus is a book about Christian living and putting God's basic principles into action. Paul had been ministering with Titus in Crete, but he had left Titus there to straighten out a particular problem. False teachers had come into the church and were causing havoc. As an antidote, Paul instructed Titus to appoint elders/overseers in each of the churches. These men would teach right doctrine and refute false doctrine.

But what are these overseers to be like? Why is godliness so important? Why is false teaching such a big deal? What is the relationship between a person's doctrine and their daily Christian living? All these questions and more are answered in this practical little letter to Titus.

You might like to use this prayer (or your own variation of it) before each of the next 20 studies:

Heavenly Father,
Thank you for sending your Son Jesus into the world. Thank you that because of his life, death and resurrection, my problem with sin has been dealt with and my eternal future has been made secure. I pray that you will help me to learn from Jesus and to become more like him through your enabling Spirit. May I never let anything get in the way of following him. In Jesus' name I pray,
Amen.

NB: Tick the box when you've completed each study ✓

READING 1   TITUS 1:1-4

Paul, a servant of God and an apostle of Jesus Christ, for the sake of the faith of God's elect and their knowledge of the truth, which accords with godliness, ² in hope of eternal life, which God, who never lies, promised before the ages began ³ and at the proper time manifested in his word through the preaching with which I have been entrusted by the command of God our Savior;
⁴ To Titus, my true child in a common faith:
Grace and peace from God the Father and Christ Jesus our Savior.

1. Why do you think Paul describes himself as a servant of God (v. 1)?

2. What two reasons does Paul give for God appointing him to be an apostle (v. 1)?

3. What is the relationship between knowing the truth and living a godly life (v. 1)?

PONDER What would you say to a friend who says that s/he believes the gospel, but who is not displaying a godly lifestyle (cf. Rom 6:1-4[1])?

PRAYER IDEAS Ask God to help you show the truth of the gospel in your daily life.

READING 2   TITUS 1:1-4

Paul, a servant of God and an apostle of Jesus Christ, for the sake of the faith of God's elect and their knowledge of the truth, which accords with godliness, [2] in hope of eternal life, which God, who never lies, promised before the ages began [3] and at the proper time manifested in his word through the preaching with which I have been entrusted by the command of God our Savior;
 [4] To Titus, my true child in a common faith: Grace and peace from God the Father and Christ Jesus our Savior.

1. What exactly did God promise before the beginning of time (v. 2)?

2. How did Paul communicate this gospel message (v. 3)?

3. Why is the public proclamation of the gospel so important?

PONDER God does not lie (v. 2). When he promises something, he always delivers. How certain can you be that you have eternal life (cf. Phil 1:6;[2] John 5:24[3])?

PRAYER IDEAS Thank God for the sure and certain hope you have through the gospel.

READING 3   TITUS 1:5-9

This is why I left you in Crete, so that you might put what remained into order, and appoint elders in every town as I directed you— [6] if anyone is above reproach, the husband of one wife, and his children are believers and not open to the charge of debauchery or insubordination. [7] For an overseer, as God's steward, must be above reproach. He must not be arrogant or quick-tempered or a drunkard or violent or greedy for gain, [8] but hospitable, a lover of good, self-controlled, upright, holy, and disciplined. [9] He must hold firm to the trustworthy word as taught, so that he may be able to give

---

1. What shall we say then? Are we to continue in sin that grace may abound? [2] By no means! How can we who died to sin still live in it? [3] Do you not know that all of us who have been baptized into Christ Jesus were baptized into his death? [4] We were buried therefore with him by baptism into death, in order that, just as Christ was raised from the dead by the glory of the Father, we too might walk in newness of life.
2. And I am sure of this, that he who began a good work in you will bring it to completion at the day of Jesus Christ.
3. Truly, truly, I say to you, whoever hears my word and believes him who sent me has eternal life. He does not come into judgment, but has passed from death to life.

instruction in sound doctrine and also to rebuke those who contradict it.

1. *Paul had been ministering with Titus in Crete, but had left him there to complete a particular task. What was it (v. 5)?*

2. *Verses 5-9 contain examples of the sorts of qualities that should be displayed in the life of people who serve as overseers/elders. Which ones stand out to you as being particularly important? Why?*

3. *What other qualities would you expect to see in an overseer?*

PONDER In 1 Timothy 3:1,[4] Paul states that if anyone aspires to the office of overseer, he desires a noble task. Is this role something that you should be considering seriously?

PRAYER IDEAS Ask God to raise up more people who are willing to serve as overseers. Pray for the ones in your church: ask God to help them to exemplify the qualities in this passage.

READING 4   1 TIMOTHY 3:1-7

The saying is trustworthy: If anyone aspires to the office of overseer, he desires a noble task. [2] Therefore an overseer must be above reproach, the husband of one wife, sober-minded, self-controlled, respectable, hospitable, able to teach, [3] not a drunkard, not violent but gentle, not quarrelsome, not a lover of money. [4] He must manage his own household well, with all dignity keeping his children submissive, [5] for if someone does not know how to manage his own household, how will he care for God's church? [6] He must not be a recent convert, or he may become puffed up with conceit and fall into the condemnation of the devil. [7] Moreover, he must be well thought of by outsiders, so that

he may not fall into disgrace, into a snare of the devil.

1. *In this passage, Paul writes to Timothy about the sorts of things that should characterize an overseer. Why do you think Paul describes being an overseer as a "noble task" (v. 1)?*

2. *What similarities and differences do you see between this passage and Titus 1:5-9?[5]*

---

4. The saying is trustworthy: If anyone aspires to the office of overseer, he desires a noble task.
5. This is why I left you in Crete, so that you might put what remained into order, and appoint elders in every town as I directed you— [6] if anyone is above reproach, the husband of one wife, and his children are believers and not open to the charge of debauchery or insubordination. [7] For an overseer,

as God's steward, must be above reproach. He must not be arrogant or quick-tempered or a drunkard or violent or greedy for gain, [8] but hospitable, a lover of good, self-controlled, upright, holy, and disciplined. [9] He must hold firm to the trustworthy word as taught, so that he may be able to give instruction in sound doctrine and also to rebuke those who contradict it.

3. *What particular ability or skill must an overseer possess (v. 2)?*

PONDER Does God 'call' someone to be an overseer or is it a human desire (v. 1)?

PRAYER IDEAS Ask God to help the overseers in your church to reflect the character of the Lord Jesus increasingly so that they are good role models for your congregation.

READING 5   TITUS 1:5-9

This is why I left you in Crete, so that you might put what remained into order, and appoint elders in every town as I directed you— [6] if anyone is above reproach, the husband of one wife, and his children are believers and not open to the charge of debauchery or insubordination. [7] For an overseer, as God's steward, must be above reproach. He must not be arrogant or quick-tempered or a drunkard or violent or greedy for gain, [8] but hospitable, a lover of good, self-controlled, upright, holy, and disciplined. [9] He must hold firm to the trustworthy word as taught, so that he may be able to give instruction in sound doctrine and also to rebuke those who contradict it.

1. *In Titus 1, Paul contrasts two groups of people in the church: the overseers (vv. 5-9) and the false teachers (vv. 10-16[6]). Why do you think it is important for an overseer to "hold firm to the trustworthy word as taught" (v. 9)?*

2. *What particular responsibilities does an overseer have (v. 9)?*

3. *How do you think the behaviour of an overseer's family could add to or subtract from an overseer's ministry (v. 6)? Why?*

PONDER Do you think an overseer could continue in this role if his life was not consistently above reproach? What should a congregation do if this happens?

PRAYER IDEAS Ask God to help the overseers in your church to live blameless lives that do not bring the gospel into disrepute.

---

6. For there are many who are insubordinate, empty talkers and deceivers, especially those of the circumcision party. [11] They must be silenced, since they are upsetting whole families by teaching for shameful gain what they ought not to teach. [12] One of the Cretans, a prophet of their own, said, "Cretans are always liars, evil beasts, lazy gluttons." [13] This testimony is true. Therefore rebuke them sharply, that they may be sound in the faith, [14] not devoting themselves to Jewish myths and the commands of people who turn away from the truth. [15] To the pure, all things are pure, but to the defiled and unbelieving, nothing is pure; but both their minds and their consciences are defiled. [16] They profess to know God, but they deny him by their works. They are detestable, disobedient, unfit for any good work.

TITUS

et the elders who rule well be considered worthy of double honor, especially those who labor in preaching and teaching. ¹⁸ For the Scripture says, "You shall not muzzle an ox when it treads out the grain," and, "The laborer deserves his wages." ¹⁹ Do not admit a charge against an elder except on the evidence of two or three witnesses. ²⁰ As for those who persist in sin, rebuke them in the presence of all, so that the rest may stand in fear. ²¹ In the presence of God and of Christ Jesus and of the elect angels I charge you to keep these rules without prejudging, doing nothing from partiality. ²² Do not be hasty in the laying on of hands, nor take part in the sins of others; keep yourself pure.

1. *No doubt that over the past few readings, you've seen that being an overseer involves great responsibility and high standards of personal Christian living. But the church has a responsibility towards their overseers as well. How are they to regard them (v. 17; cf. 1 Thess 5:12-13⁷)?*

2. *In verse 18, Paul quotes Deuteronomy 25:4⁸ and Luke 10:7.⁹ What do these verses mean in their original context? What point is Paul making in verse 18?*

3. *How else are overseers to be treated (vv. 19-20)?*

PONDER How fairly is your congregation treating your overseers at the moment? How fairly are you treating them?

PRAYER IDEAS Thank God for the overseers he has given your congregation. Ask God to help you to treat them with honour, respect and fairness.

ISAIAH 13-27

TEN COMMANDMENTS

---

7. We ask you, brothers, to respect those who labor among you and are over you in the Lord and admonish you, ¹³ and to esteem them very highly in love because of their work. Be at peace among yourselves.

8. "If there is a dispute between men and they come into court and the judges decide between them, acquitting the innocent and condemning the guilty, ² then if the guilty man deserves to be beaten, the judge shall cause him to lie down and be beaten in his presence with a number of stripes in proportion to his offense. ³ Forty stripes may be given him, but not more, lest, if one should go on to beat him with more stripes than these, your brother be degraded in your sight.

⁴ "You shall not muzzle an ox when it is treading out the grain.

⁵ "If brothers dwell together, and one of them dies and has no son, the wife of the dead man shall not be married outside the family to a stranger. Her husband's brother shall go in to her and take her as his wife and perform the duty of

a husband's brother to her. ⁶ And the first son whom she bears shall succeed to the name of his dead brother, that his name may not be blotted out of Israel.

9. After this the Lord appointed seventy-two others and sent them on ahead of him, two by two, into every town and place where he himself was about to go. ² And he said to them, "The harvest is plentiful, but the laborers are few. Therefore pray earnestly to the Lord of the harvest to send out laborers into his harvest. ³ Go your way; behold, I am sending you out as lambs in the midst of wolves. ⁴ Carry no moneybag, no knapsack, no sandals, and greet no one on the road. ⁵ Whatever house you enter, first say, 'Peace be to this house!' ⁶ And if a son of peace is there, your peace will rest upon him. But if not, it will return to you. ⁷ And remain in the same house, eating and drinking what they provide, for the laborer deserves his wages. Do not go from house to house. ⁸ Whenever you enter a town and they receive you, eat what is set before you. ⁹ Heal the sick in it and say to them, 'The kingdom of God has come near to you.'"

And James and John, the sons of Zebedee, came up to him and said to him, "Teacher, we want you to do for us whatever we ask of you." 36 And he said to them, "What do you want me to do for you?" 37 And they said to him, "Grant us to sit, one at your right hand and one at your left, in your glory." 38 Jesus said to them, "You do not know what you are asking. Are you able to drink the cup that I drink, or to be baptized with the baptism with which I am baptized?" 39 And they said to him, "We are able." And Jesus said to them, "The cup that I drink you will drink, and with the baptism with which I am baptized, you will be baptized, 40 but to sit at my right hand or at my left is not mine to grant, but it is for those for whom it has been prepared." 41 And when the ten heard it, they began to be indignant at James and John. 42 And Jesus called them to him and said to them, "You know that those who are considered rulers of the Gentiles lord it over them, and their great ones exercise authority over them. 43 But it shall not be so among you. But whoever would be great among you must be your servant, 44 and whoever would be first among you must be slave of all."

1. What was wrong with James and John's request? What do you think was the motivation behind it?

2. What does Jesus say is the secular mindset regarding leadership (v. 42)? What sort of examples of this sort of leadership can you think of?

3. What does Jesus say should be the Christian's mindset to leadership (vv. 42-3)? How did Jesus model this?

PONDER What type of leader do you think you are: one who rules or one who serves? What changes could you make to become more like a servant leader?

PRAYER IDEAS Confess to God the times when you have been a selfish leader rather than a servant leader. Ask God to increase your servant heart so that you will serve others willingly and sacrificially.

For there are many who are insubordinate, empty talkers and deceivers, especially those of the circumcision party. 11 They must be silenced, since they are upsetting whole families by teaching for shameful gain what they ought not to teach. 12 One of the Cretans, a prophet of their own, said, "Cretans are always liars, evil beasts, lazy gluttons." 13 This testimony is true. Therefore rebuke them sharply, that they may be sound in the faith, 14 not devoting themselves to Jewish myths and the commands of people who turn away from the truth. 15 To the pure, all things are pure, but to the defiled and unbelieving, nothing is pure; but both their minds and their consciences are defiled. 16 They profess to know God, but they deny him by their works. They are detestable, disobedient, unfit for any good work.

1. What sorts of things do you learn about the false teachers who have infiltrated the church?

2. Why is false teaching such a big deal? What are the overseers to do about it (vv. 11, 13-14)?

3. Why is it so important for a church to have overseers who teach right doctrine and correct false doctrine?

PONDER What effect might it have on a church if their overseers didn't refute false teaching or, even worse, were false teachers themselves?

PRAYER IDEAS Ask God to help you to not be led astray by false teaching. Ask God to help the overseers in your church to give instruction in sound doctrine and to rebuke those who contradict it.

READING 9   TITUS 1:10-16

For there are many who are insubordinate, empty talkers and deceivers, especially those of the circumcision party. ¹¹ They must be silenced, since they are upsetting whole families by teaching for shameful gain what they ought not to teach. ¹² One of the Cretans, a prophet of their own, said, "Cretans are always liars, evil beasts, lazy gluttons." ¹³ This testimony is true. Therefore rebuke them sharply, that they may be sound in the faith, ¹⁴ not devoting themselves to Jewish myths and the commands of people who turn away from the truth. ¹⁵ To the pure, all things are pure, but to the defiled and unbelieving, nothing is pure; but both their minds and their consciences are defiled. ¹⁶ They profess to know God, but they deny him by their works. They are detestable, disobedient, unfit for any good work.

1. The teachings of the circumcision party continued to crop up throughout Paul's ministry (see pointer). What do you learn about them from Galatians 6:10-16?[10]

2. Verse 15 suggests the circumcision party was quite legalistic. Read 1 Timothy 4:3-5.[11] What sorts of things were they legalistic about?

---

10. So then, as we have opportunity, let us do good to everyone, and especially to those who are of the household of faith.
¹¹ See with what large letters I am writing to you with my own hand. ¹² It is those who want to make a good showing in the flesh who would force you to be circumcised, and only in order that they may not be persecuted for the cross of Christ. ¹³ For even those who are circumcised do not themselves keep the law, but they desire to have you circumcised that they may boast in your flesh. ¹⁴ But far be it from me to boast except in the cross of our Lord Jesus Christ, by which the world has been crucified to me, and I to the world. ¹⁵ For neither circumcision counts for anything, nor uncircumcision, but a new creation. ¹⁶ And as for all who walk by this rule, peace and mercy be upon them, and upon the Israel of God.
11. ... who forbid marriage and require abstinence from foods that God created to be received with thanksgiving by those who believe and know the truth. ⁴ For everything created by God is good, and nothing is to be rejected if it is received with thanksgiving, ⁵ for it is made holy by the word of God and prayer.

TITUS

ISAIAH 13-27

TEN COMMANDMENTS

3. How does Paul counter their legalism (v. 15)?

PONDER What modern-day examples of legalism have you come across?

PRAYER IDEAS Ask God to give you a deep grasp of the grace that is found in Christ. Also ask him for the strength to resist the temptation to give this grace up.

POINTERS v. 10: "circumcision party" is code for Jews and (most likely) Jewish Christians who wanted all other Christians to wear the badges of Judaism—particularly circumcision. They are probably the same group that Paul refutes in Galatians.
v. 14: "Jewish myths" most likely refers to stories spun out of the Old Testament that claimed to impart special knowledge.

READING 10   TITUS 2:1-10 (FOCUSING ON VERSES 1-2) ■

But as for you, teach what accords with sound doctrine. ² Older men are to be sober-minded, dignified, self-controlled, sound in faith, in love, and in steadfastness. ³ Older women likewise are to be reverent in behavior, not slanderers or slaves to much wine. They are to teach what is good, ⁴ and so train the young women to love their husbands and children, ⁵ to be self-controlled, pure, working at home, kind, and submissive to their own husbands, that the word of God may not be reviled. ⁶ Likewise, urge the younger men to be self-controlled. ⁷ Show yourself in all respects to be a model of good works, and in your teaching show integrity, dignity, ⁸ and sound speech that cannot be condemned, so that an opponent may be put to shame, having nothing evil to say about us. ⁹ Slaves are to be submissive to their own masters in everything; they are to be well-pleasing, not argumentative, ¹⁰ not pilfering, but showing all good faith, so that in everything they may adorn the doctrine of God our Savior.

1. Titus is to "teach what accords with sound doctrine" (v. 1). Why do you think Paul reminds him of this here?

2. "Right doctrine leads to right behaviour." Do you agree or disagree? Why?

3. Titus 2:1-10 is about the different groups of people in churches putting their doctrine into practice. In verse 2, Paul addresses the older men. What sorts of things should characterize their behaviour?

PONDER Can people tell you're a Christian by the way you live?

PRAYER IDEAS Ask God to help you speak and live out the truth of the gospel.

But as for you, teach what accords with sound doctrine. 2 Older men are to be sober-minded, dignified, self-controlled, sound in faith, in love, and in steadfastness. 3 Older women likewise are to be reverent in behavior, not slanderers or slaves to much wine. They are to teach what is good, 4 and so train the young women to love their husbands and children, 5 to be self-controlled, pure, working at home, kind, and submissive to their own husbands, that the word of God may not be reviled. 6 Likewise, urge the younger men to be self-controlled. 7 Show yourself in all respects to be a model of good works, and in your teaching show integrity, dignity, 8 and sound speech that cannot be condemned, so that an opponent may be put to shame, having nothing evil to say about us. 9 Slaves are to be submissive to their own masters in everything; they are to be well-pleasing, not argumentative, 10 not pilfering, but showing all good faith, so that in everything they may adorn the doctrine of God our Savior.

1. What should Titus teach the older women (vv. 3-4)?

2. What should the older women train the younger women to do (vv. 4-5)?

3. What are some examples of young women living in a way that causes the word of God to be reviled?

PONDER Paul wants young women to focus on their husbands and children. How might this conflict with current social expectations? What can other Christians do to help them?

PRAYER IDEAS Thank God for the older women in your church. Ask him to help them live godly lives and teach the younger women in your church. In addition, ask him to help the married younger women to make wise decisions as they seek to live godly lives while keeping their focus on their husbands and children.

But as for you, teach what accords with sound doctrine. 2 Older men are to be sober-minded, dignified, self-controlled, sound in faith, in love, and in steadfastness. 3 Older women likewise are to be reverent in behavior, not slanderers or slaves to much wine. They are to teach what is good, 4 and so train the young women to love their husbands and children, 5 to be self-controlled, pure, working at home, kind, and submissive to their own husbands, that the word of God may not be reviled. 6 Likewise, urge the younger men to be self-controlled. 7 Show yourself in all respects to be a model of good works, and in your teaching show integrity, dignity, 8 and sound speech that cannot be condemned, so that an opponent may be put to shame, having nothing evil to say about us. 9 Slaves are to be submissive to their own masters in everything; they are to

TITUS

ISAIAH 13-27

TEN COMMANDMENTS

be well-pleasing, not argumentative, [10] not pilfering, but showing all good faith, so that in everything they may adorn the doctrine of God our Savior.

1. What do you think it would mean for the young men to be self-controlled (v. 6)?

2. How is Titus to behave as he teaches the young men (vv. 7-8)?

3. Why is Titus to teach in this manner?

What outcome could he expect to see?

PONDER In verse 7, Paul tells Titus to set the young men an example "in all respects" by doing what is good. List five areas in which your church leaders could be good examples to your congregation.

PRAYER IDEAS Ask God to help the leaders of your church to exhibit godliness as they teach the younger men. Also ask him to enable the young men to live self-controlled lives.

POINTER v. 7: The word 'model' can also be translated 'prototype' or 'pattern'.

READING 13   TITUS 2:1-10 (FOCUSING ON VERSES 9-10)

But as for you, teach what accords with sound doctrine. [2] Older men are to be sober-minded, dignified, self-controlled, sound in faith, in love, and in steadfastness. [3] Older women likewise are to be reverent in behavior, not slanderers or slaves to much wine. They are to teach what is good, [4] and so train the young women to love their husbands and children, [5] to be self-controlled, pure, working at home, kind, and submissive to their own husbands, that the word of God may not be reviled. [6] Likewise, urge the younger men to be self-controlled. [7] Show yourself in all respects to be a model of good works, and in your teaching show integrity, dignity, [8] and sound speech that cannot be condemned, so that an opponent may be put to shame, having nothing evil to say about us. [9] Slaves are to be submissive to their own masters in everything; they are to be well-pleasing, not argumentative, [10] not

pilfering, but showing all good faith, so that in everything they may adorn the doctrine of God our Savior.

1. What is Paul's primary concern regarding the behaviour of slaves (v. 10; cf. vv. 5, 8)?

2. How can slaves relate to their masters positively?

3. Titus is continually called upon to teach (vv. 1, 7). What must he be careful to do as he carries out this important role (cf. 1 Tim 4:16[12])?

---

12. Keep a close watch on yourself and on the teaching. Persist in this, for by so doing you will save both yourself and your hearers.

PONDER Although few of us are in a master-slave relationship, many of us are employees. How can your conduct at work bring credit to/discredit the gospel?

PRAYER IDEAS Ask God to enable Christians you know to bring credit to the gospel through their conduct at work. Ask God to make you sensitive to how you are perceived in the workplace.

READING 14   TITUS 2:11-15 (FOCUSING ON VERSES 11-13)

For the grace of God has appeared, bringing salvation for all people, [12] training us to renounce ungodliness and worldly passions, and to live self-controlled, upright, and godly lives in the present age, [13] waiting for our blessed hope, the appearing of the glory of our great God and Savior Jesus Christ, [14] who gave himself for us to redeem us from all lawlessness and to purify for himself a people for his own possession who are zealous for good works.

[15] Declare these things; exhort and rebuke with all authority. Let no one disregard you.

1. Who is God's offer of salvation for (v. 11)?

2. What two events involving salvation does

Paul refer to in verses 11 and 13? How are they related?

3. How does your salvation affect the way you live now (v. 12)?

PONDER What will it mean for you to "renounce ungodliness and worldly passions" and live a "self-controlled, upright, and godly" life (v. 12)?

PRAYER IDEAS Thank God for sending the Lord Jesus Christ to be your saviour, and for allowing you to receive and believe the gospel message. Ask him to help you to "renounce ungodliness and worldly passions" and live a "self-controlled, upright, and godly" life (v. 12).

READING 15   TITUS 2:11-15 (FOCUSING ON VERSE 14)

For the grace of God has appeared, bringing salvation for all people, [12] training us to renounce ungodliness and worldly passions, and to live self-controlled, upright, and godly lives in the present age, [13] waiting for our blessed hope, the appearing of the glory of our great God and Savior Jesus Christ, [14] who gave himself for us to redeem us from all lawlessness and to purify for himself a people for his own possession who are zealous for

good works.

[15] Declare these things; exhort and rebuke with all authority. Let no one disregard you.

1. What has Jesus done for you (v. 14)? What do these things mean?

2. What were you like before Jesus redeemed and purified you?

3. How are you to live now?

PONDER Paul wants us to look back at the grace shown to us at Jesus' first appearance (v. 11) and look forward to the glorious future when he will appear again (v. 13). How will these two events affect the way you live now?

PRAYER IDEAS Reflect again on the enormity of Jesus' redeeming sacrifice for you on the cross. Thank him for it, and ask him to help you to live a life free of wickedness, "zealous for good works" (v. 14).

READING 16   TITUS 3:1-2

Remind them to be submissive to rulers and authorities, to be obedient, to be ready for every good work, ² to speak evil of no one, to avoid quarreling, to be gentle, and to show perfect courtesy toward all people.

1. List the things that Titus is to remind the people to do.

2. How does this list compare with Romans 13:1-7?¹³

3. How does this list compare with the false teachers in Titus 1:16?¹⁴

PONDER The book of Titus was written at a time when the state viewed the church in a positive light. This will not always be the case. In what areas do you struggle to obey the law? Under what circumstances could a Christian choose not to be "submissive to rulers and authorities" (v. 1)?

PRAYER IDEAS Ask God to help you submit to the laws of the land in which you are living, even if they might seem ill-conceived. Ask him to give you true humility in your interactions with others.

---

13. Let every person be subject to the governing authorities. For there is no authority except from God, and those that exist have been instituted by God. ² Therefore whoever resists the authorities resists what God has appointed, and those who resist will incur judgment. ³ For rulers are not a terror to good conduct, but to bad. Would you have no fear of the one who is in authority? Then do what is good, and you will receive his approval, ⁴ for he is God's servant for your good. But if you do wrong, be afraid, for he does not bear the sword in vain. For he is the servant of God, an avenger who carries out God's wrath on the wrongdoer. ⁵ Therefore one must be in subjection, not only to avoid God's wrath but also for the sake of conscience. ⁶ For because of this you also pay taxes, for the authorities are ministers of God, attending to this very thing. ⁷ Pay to all what is owed to them: taxes to whom taxes are owed, revenue to whom revenue is owed, respect to whom respect is owed, honor to whom honor is owed.

14. They profess to know God, but they deny him by their works. They are detestable, disobedient, unfit for any good work.

For we ourselves were once foolish, disobedient, led astray, slaves to various passions and pleasures, passing our days in malice and envy, hated by others and hating one another. ⁴ But when the goodness and loving kindness of God our Savior appeared, ⁵ he saved us, not because of works done by us in righteousness ...

1. Why do you need salvation (v. 3)?

2. Who is ultimately responsible for your salvation (v. 4)?

3. Why did God save you (v. 4-5a)?

PONDER What tempts you to think that you contributed to your salvation in some way?

PRAYER IDEAS Ask God to keep changing you by his Holy Spirit so that you are less like how you were before you became a Christian and more like Jesus.

... but according to his own mercy, by the washing of regeneration and renewal of the Holy Spirit, ⁶ whom he poured out on us richly through Jesus Christ our Savior, ⁷ so that being justified by his grace we might become heirs according to the hope of eternal life. ⁸ The saying is trustworthy, and I want you to insist on these things, so that those who have believed in God may be careful to devote themselves to good works. These things are excellent and profitable for people.

1. How did God save you, according to verses 5b-6? Who was involved?

2. What do you gain by being declared righteous by God (vv. 5-7)?

3. Paul makes the same point in verse 8 that he did in verses 1-2.¹⁵ Why does he do this?

---

15. Remind them to be submissive to rulers and authorities, to be obedient, to be ready for every good work, ² to speak evil of no one, to avoid quarreling, to be gentle, and to show perfect courtesy toward all people.

PONDER In Titus 3:1-8,[16] Paul ties the gospel with Christian conduct. What's the connection?

PRAYER IDEAS Ask God to help you devote yourself to doing what is good in his sight so that others might see Christ in a positive light.

But avoid foolish controversies, genealogies, dissensions, and quarrels about the law, for they are unprofitable and worthless. [10] As for a person who stirs up division, after warning him once and then twice, have nothing more to do with him, [11] knowing that such a person is warped and sinful; he is self-condemned.

1. What does Paul say Titus and the Cretans should avoid (v. 9)? Why?

2. How does this behaviour compare to how Christians ought to live in verses 1-2[17] and 8?[18]

3. How is Titus to deal with these false teachers/quarrelers (v. 10)? What do

you think is the reasoning behind Paul's instructions?

4. What do you think is the false teacher's/ quarreller's standing before God (v. 11; cf. 1:15-16[19])? What is the relationship between their beliefs and their actions?

PONDER Where do you see false teachers making a negative impression on the church and Christianity?

PRAYER IDEAS Ask God to help you be discerning about whether to engage in controversies, theological arguments and other points of division.

---

16. Remind them to be submissive to rulers and authorities, to be obedient, to be ready for every good work, [2] to speak evil of no one, to avoid quarreling, to be gentle, and to show perfect courtesy toward all people. [3] For we ourselves were once foolish, disobedient, led astray, slaves to various passions and pleasures, passing our days in malice and envy, hated by others and hating one another. [4] But when the goodness and loving kindness of God our Savior appeared, [5] he saved us, not because of works done by us in righteousness, but according to his own mercy, by the washing of regeneration and renewal of the Holy Spirit, [6] whom he poured out on us richly through Jesus Christ our Savior, [7] so that being justified by his grace we might become heirs according to the hope of eternal life. [8] The saying is trustworthy, and I want you to insist on these things, so that those who have believed in God may be careful

to devote themselves to good works. These things are excellent and profitable for people.

17. Remind them to be submissive to rulers and authorities, to be obedient, to be ready for every good work, [2] to speak evil of no one, to avoid quarreling, to be gentle, and to show perfect courtesy toward all people.

18. The saying is trustworthy, and I want you to insist on these things, so that those who have believed in God may be careful to devote themselves to good works. These things are excellent and profitable for people.

19. To the pure, all things are pure, but to the defiled and unbelieving, nothing is pure; but both their minds and their consciences are defiled. [16] They profess to know God, but they deny him by their works. They are detestable, disobedient, unfit for any good work.

When I send Artemas or Tychicus to you, do your best to come to me at Nicopolis, for I have decided to spend the winter there. [13] Do your best to speed Zenas the lawyer and Apollos on their way; see that they lack nothing. [14] And let our people learn to devote themselves to good works, so as to help cases of urgent need, and not be unfruitful.

[15] All who are with me send greetings to you. Greet those who love us in the faith. Grace be with you all.

1. What instructions does Paul give to Timothy—particularly concerning "our people" (v. 14)?

2. What does this tell you about Paul's focus (cf. 2:7;[20] 3:1, 8[21])?

3. What is the point of appropriate Christian conduct (v. 14)?

PONDER What changes can you make to "devote [yourself] to good works" more (v. 14)?

PRAYER IDEAS Ask God to make you a blessing to other Christians in your diligence to provide for the needs of others—whether those in your church or further afield.

20. Show yourself in all respects to be a model of good works, and in your teaching show integrity, dignity ...
21. Remind them to be submissive to rulers and authorities, to be obedient, to be ready for every good work ... [8] The saying is trustworthy, and I want you to insist on these things, so that those who have believed in God may be careful to devote themselves to good works. These things are excellent and profitable for people.

ISAIAH 13-27

INTRODUCTION

This section of Isaiah seems terribly gloomy as it is filled with prophecies regarding God's judgement on both the nations surrounding Israel and on the nation of Israel itself for their rebellion against him and their flagrant idolatry. However, these chapters also contain a great message of hope. Because God is faithful, he will bring salvation to his people, and usher in a new age when they will rejoice and sing his praises, and death will be defeated once and for all. Ultimately, these prophecies of judgement and salvation are fulfilled in the person and work of Jesus Christ.

You might like to use this prayer (or your own variation of it) before each of the next 20 studies:

Heavenly Father,
Thank you for being faithful to your promises, and righteous and holy in your judgements. Thank you for loving and caring for me, cleansing me from my sin and making me one of your children through Jesus' death and resurrection. Please help me to live a life glorifying to you as I wait for Jesus' return and the glorious future that you have promised in which people from all nations will gather together to feast and praise your name.
Amen.

READING 21   ISAIAH 1:1 BACKGROUND

The vision of Isaiah the son of Amoz, which he saw concerning Judah and Jerusalem in the days of Uzziah, Jotham, Ahaz, and Hezekiah, kings of Judah.

1. What does Isaiah 1:1 tell you about the prophet Isaiah?

2. Skim read 2 Kings 18-20 in the appendix (pp. 65-69), and jot down very brief notes on the main events of Hezekiah's reign. How does his story end?

PONDER Why do you think the book of Isaiah is described as a 'vision' (v. 1)? What possible meanings might this word have in this context?

PRAYER IDEAS Thank God for causing his plans and purposes for the world to be centred in Jesus and in the people he has gathered to himself in Jesus. Thank God for the future he has in store—the new Jerusalem to come where we will be citizens. Ask him to help you to see his vision for the world and to change your life accordingly as you read the book of Isaiah.

READING 22   ISAIAH 13

The oracle concerning Babylon which Isaiah the son of Amoz saw.

2 On a bare hill raise a signal;
  cry aloud to them;
wave the hand for them to enter
  the gates of the nobles.
3 I myself have commanded my consecrated
    ones,
  and have summoned my mighty men to
      execute my anger,
  my proudly exulting ones.

4 The sound of a tumult is on the mountains
  as of a great multitude!
The sound of an uproar of kingdoms,
  of nations gathering together!
The LORD of hosts is mustering
  a host for battle.
5 They come from a distant land,
  from the end of the heavens,
the LORD and the weapons of his indignation,
  to destroy the whole land.

6 Wail, for the day of the LORD is near;
  as destruction from the Almighty it will
      come!
7 Therefore all hands will be feeble,
  and every human heart will melt.
8 They will be dismayed:
  pangs and agony will seize them;
  they will be in anguish like a woman in
      labor.
They will look aghast at one another;
  their faces will be aflame.

9 Behold, the day of the LORD comes,

  cruel, with wrath and fierce anger,
to make the land a desolation
  and to destroy its sinners from it.
10 For the stars of the heavens and their
      constellations
  will not give their light;
the sun will be dark at its rising,
  and the moon will not shed its light.
11 I will punish the world for its evil,
  and the wicked for their iniquity;
I will put an end to the pomp of the
      arrogant,
  and lay low the pompous pride of the
      ruthless.
12 I will make people more rare than fine
      gold,
  and mankind than the gold of Ophir.
13 Therefore I will make the heavens tremble,
  and the earth will be shaken out of its
      place,
at the wrath of the LORD of hosts
  in the day of his fierce anger.
14 And like a hunted gazelle,
  or like sheep with none to gather them,
each will turn to his own people,
  and each will flee to his own land.
15 Whoever is found will be thrust through,
  and whoever is caught will fall by the
      sword.
16 Their infants will be dashed in pieces
  before their eyes;
their houses will be plundered
  and their wives ravished.

17 Behold, I am stirring up the Medes against
      them,
  who have no regard for silver

and do not delight in gold.
18 Their bows will slaughter the young men;
    they will have no mercy on the fruit of
        the womb;
their eyes will not pity children.
19 And Babylon, the glory of kingdoms,
    the splendor and pomp of the Chaldeans,
will be like Sodom and Gomorrah
    when God overthrew them.
20 It will never be inhabited
    or lived in for all generations;
no Arab will pitch his tent there;
    no shepherds will make their flocks lie
        down there.
21 But wild animals will lie down there,
    and their houses will be full of howling
        creatures;
there ostriches will dwell,
    and there wild goats will dance.
22 Hyenas will cry in its towers,
    and jackals in the pleasant palaces;
its time is close at hand
    and its days will not be prolonged.

*1. What does God promise will happen to
Babylon?*

*2. What do you think would have been
Israel's response to this passage?*

*3. How is God's judgement here (and
elsewhere in Scripture) an expression of
his justice?*

PONDER Why do you think God takes evil so
seriously? Is it contradictory for him to deal
with evil by using evil?

PRAYER IDEAS Thank God for not letting
evil flourish forever. Thank him for setting
aside a day when justice will be exercised fully
and finally.

POINTER Although Babylon doesn't replace
Assyria as the primary world power until
550 BC, Isaiah 39 [22] reveals that Israel and
Isaiah were well aware of Babylon's existence
and its threat to Judah's security—a threat
even more serious than Assyria.

READING 23   ISAIAH 14:1-23 ▮

For the LORD will have compassion on Jacob
and will again choose Israel, and will set
them in their own land, and sojourners will
join them and will attach themselves to the
house of Jacob. 2 And the peoples will take
them and bring them to their place, and the

---

22. At that time Merodach-baladan the son of Baladan, king
of Babylon, sent envoys with letters and a present to Hezekiah,
for he heard that he had been sick and had recovered. 2 And
Hezekiah welcomed them gladly. And he showed them his
treasure house, the silver, the gold, the spices, the precious oil,
his whole armory, all that was found in his storehouses. There
was nothing in his house or in all his realm that Hezekiah
did not show them. 3 Then Isaiah the prophet came to King
Hezekiah, and said to him, "What did these men say? And from
where did they come to you?" Hezekiah said, "They have come
to me from a far country, from Babylon." 4 He said, "What have
they seen in your house?" Hezekiah answered, "They have seen
all that is in my house. There is nothing in my storehouses that
I did not show them."
    5 Then Isaiah said to Hezekiah, "Hear the word of the LORD
of hosts: 6 Behold, the days are coming, when all that is in your
house, and that which your fathers have stored up till this day,
shall be carried to Babylon. Nothing shall be left, says the LORD.
7 And some of your own sons, who will come from you, whom
you will father, shall be taken away, and they shall be eunuchs
in the palace of the king of Babylon." 8 Then said Hezekiah to
Isaiah, "The word of the LORD that you have spoken is good." For
he thought, "There will be peace and security in my days."

house of Israel will possess them in the Lord's land as male and female slaves. They will take captive those who were their captors, and rule over those who oppressed them.

3 When the Lord has given you rest from your pain and turmoil and the hard service with which you were made to serve, 4 you will take up this taunt against the king of Babylon:

"How the oppressor has ceased,
　　the insolent fury ceased!
5 The Lord has broken the staff of the wicked,
　　the scepter of rulers,
6 that struck the peoples in wrath
　　with unceasing blows,
that ruled the nations in anger
　　with unrelenting persecution.
7 The whole earth is at rest and quiet;
　　they break forth into singing.
8 The cypresses rejoice at you,
　　the cedars of Lebanon, saying,
'Since you were laid low,
　　no woodcutter comes up against us.'
9 Sheol beneath is stirred up
　　to meet you when you come;
it rouses the shades to greet you,
　　all who were leaders of the earth;
it raises from their thrones
　　all who were kings of the nations.
10 All of them will answer
　　and say to you:
'You too have become as weak as we!
　　You have become like us!'
11 Your pomp is brought down to Sheol,
　　the sound of your harps;
maggots are laid as a bed beneath you,
　　and worms are your covers.

12 "How you are fallen from heaven,
　　O Day Star, son of Dawn!
How you are cut down to the ground,
　　you who laid the nations low!
13 You said in your heart,
　　'I will ascend to heaven;

above the stars of God
　　I will set my throne on high;
I will sit on the mount of assembly
　　in the far reaches of the north;
14 I will ascend above the heights of the clouds;
　　I will make myself like the Most High.'
15 But you are brought down to Sheol,
　　to the far reaches of the pit.
16 Those who see you will stare at you
　　and ponder over you:
'Is this the man who made the earth tremble,
　　who shook kingdoms,
17 who made the world like a desert
　　and overthrew its cities,
　　who did not let his prisoners go home?'
18 All the kings of the nations lie in glory,
　　each in his own tomb;
19 but you are cast out, away from your grave,
　　like a loathed branch,
clothed with the slain, those pierced by the sword,
　　who go down to the stones of the pit,
　　like a dead body trampled underfoot.
20 You will not be joined with them in burial,
　　because you have destroyed your land,
　　you have slain your people.

"May the offspring of evildoers
　　nevermore be named!
21 Prepare slaughter for his sons
　　because of the guilt of their fathers,
lest they rise and possess the earth,
　　and fill the face of the world with cities."

22 "I will rise up against them," declares the Lord of hosts, "and will cut off from Babylon name and remnant, descendants and posterity," declares the Lord. 23 "And I will make it a possession of the hedgehog, and pools of water, and I will sweep it with the broom of destruction," declares the Lord of hosts.

1. What good news does God promise Jacob (i.e. Israel)?

2. What bad news does God promise Jacob's enemies?

3. Why do you think salvation and judgement go hand in hand in the Bible?

4. What does this tell you about God?

PONDER What should be your response to both judgement and salvation?

PRAYER IDEAS Thank God for being prepared both to save and to judge. Ask him to give you a proper understanding of these twin aspects of his dealings with humanity.

POINTER v. 1: The names 'Jacob' and 'Israel' hark back to the ancient ideal of a single nation.

READING 24   ISAIAH 14:24-32

The LORD of hosts has sworn:
"As I have planned,
    so shall it be,
and as I have purposed,
    so shall it stand,
25 that I will break the Assyrian in my land,
    and on my mountains trample him
        underfoot;
and his yoke shall depart from them,
    and his burden from their shoulder."

26 This is the purpose that is purposed
        concerning the whole earth,
and this is the hand that is stretched out
    over all the nations.
27 For the LORD of hosts has purposed,
    and who will annul it?
His hand is stretched out,
    and who will turn it back?

28 In the year that King Ahaz died came this
        oracle:

29 Rejoice not, O Philistia, all of you,
    that the rod that struck you is broken,

for from the serpent's root will come forth
        an adder,
    and its fruit will be a flying fiery serpent.
30 And the firstborn of the poor will graze,
    and the needy lie down in safety;
but I will kill your root with famine,
    and your remnant it will slay.
31 Wail, O gate; cry out, O city;
    melt in fear, O Philistia, all of you!
For smoke comes out of the north,
    and there is no straggler in his ranks.

32 What will one answer the messengers of
        the nation?
"The LORD has founded Zion,
    and in her the afflicted of his people
        find refuge."

1. What does God promise the Assyrians? What does he promise the Philistines?

2. What does this tell you about those who oppose God and his people?

3. King Ahaz appears in verse 28. Why do you think Isaiah's mention of him would have tempered any sense of self-righteousness on the part of the Israelites? (Hint: see pointer.)

PONDER Why is the prospect of God's judgement humbling for both the ones being judged and the ones looking on?

PRAYER IDEAS Thank God for being so powerful, he cannot be thwarted by human opposition. Ask him to help you to be humble in the face of his righteous judgement.

POINTERS v. 25: Assyria lay to the north, far from Judah.
v. 28: King Ahaz reigned over Judah from about 735 to 715 BC. He was known for worshipping and trusting in gods other than the Lord (cf. Isa 7:1-2;[23] 2 Kgs 16:1-16 [see the appendix, p. 69]; 2 Chr 28:1-4,[24] 22-25[25]).
v. 29: Philistia lay to the east, close to Judah.

READING 25   ISAIAH 15-16

An oracle concerning Moab.

Because Ar of Moab is laid waste in a night,
    Moab is undone;
because Kir of Moab is laid waste in a night,
    Moab is undone.
2 He has gone up to the temple, and to
        Dibon,
    to the high places to weep;
over Nebo and over Medeba
    Moab wails.
On every head is baldness;
    every beard is shorn;
3 in the streets they wear sackcloth;
    on the housetops and in the squares
everyone wails and melts in tears.

4 Heshbon and Elealeh cry out;
    their voice is heard as far as Jahaz;
therefore the armed men of Moab cry
        aloud;
    his soul trembles.
5 My heart cries out for Moab;
    her fugitives flee to Zoar,
    to Eglath-shelishiyah.
For at the ascent of Luhith
    they go up weeping;
on the road to Horonaim
    they raise a cry of destruction;
6 the waters of Nimrim
    are a desolation;
the grass is withered, the vegetation fails,
    the greenery is no more.

23. In the days of Ahaz the son of Jotham, son of Uzziah, king of Judah, Rezin the king of Syria and Pekah the son of Remaliah the king of Israel came up to Jerusalem to wage war against it, but could not yet mount an attack against it. 2 When the house of David was told, "Syria is in league with Ephraim," the heart of Ahaz and the heart of his people shook as the trees of the forest shake before the wind.
24. Ahaz was twenty years old when he began to reign, and he reigned sixteen years in Jerusalem. And he did not do what was right in the eyes of the LORD, as his father David had done, 2 but he walked in the ways of the kings of Israel. He even made metal images for the Baals, 3 and he made offerings in the Valley of the Son of Hinnom and burned his sons as an offering, according to the abominations of the nations whom the LORD

drove out before the people of Israel. 4 And he sacrificed and made offerings on the high places and on the hills and under every green tree.
25. In the time of his distress he became yet more faithless to the LORD—this same King Ahaz. 23 For he sacrificed to the gods of Damascus that had defeated him and said, "Because the gods of the kings of Syria helped them, I will sacrifice to them that they may help me." But they were the ruin of him and of all Israel. 24 And Ahaz gathered together the vessels of the house of God and cut in pieces the vessels of the house of God, and he shut up the doors of the house of the LORD, and he made himself altars in every corner of Jerusalem. 25 In every city of Judah he made high places to make offerings to other gods, provoking to anger the LORD, the God of his fathers.

⁷ Therefore the abundance they have gained
  and what they have laid up
they carry away
  over the Brook of the Willows.
⁸ For a cry has gone
  around the land of Moab;
her wailing reaches to Eglaim;
  her wailing reaches to Beer-elim.
⁹ For the waters of Dibon are full of blood;
  for I will bring upon Dibon even more,
a lion for those of Moab who escape,
  for the remnant of the land.
16:1 Send the lamb to the ruler of the land,
from Sela, by way of the desert,
  to the mount of the daughter of Zion.
² Like fleeing birds,
  like a scattered nest,
so are the daughters of Moab
  at the fords of the Arnon.

³ "Give counsel;
  grant justice;
make your shade like night
  at the height of noon;
shelter the outcasts;
  do not reveal the fugitive;
⁴ let the outcasts of Moab
  sojourn among you;
be a shelter to them
  from the destroyer.
When the oppressor is no more,
  and destruction has ceased,
and he who tramples underfoot has
      vanished from the land,
⁵ then a throne will be established in
      steadfast love,
  and on it will sit in faithfulness
  in the tent of David
one who judges and seeks justice
  and is swift to do righteousness."

⁶ We have heard of the pride of Moab—
  how proud he is!—
of his arrogance, his pride, and his insolence;
  in his idle boasting he is not right.
⁷ Therefore let Moab wail for Moab,

  let everyone wail.
Mourn, utterly stricken,
  for the raisin cakes of Kir-hareseth.

⁸ For the fields of Heshbon languish,
  and the vine of Sibmah;
the lords of the nations
  have struck down its branches,
which reached to Jazer
  and strayed to the desert;
its shoots spread abroad
  and passed over the sea.
⁹ Therefore I weep with the weeping of Jazer
  for the vine of Sibmah;
I drench you with my tears,
  O Heshbon and Elealeh;
for over your summer fruit and your harvest
  the shout has ceased.
¹⁰ And joy and gladness are taken away from
      the fruitful field,
and in the vineyards no songs are sung,
  no cheers are raised;
no treader treads out wine in the presses;
  I have put an end to the shouting.
¹¹ Therefore my inner parts moan like a lyre
      for Moab,
  and my inmost self for Kir-hareseth.

¹² And when Moab presents himself, when
he wearies himself on the high place, when
he comes to his sanctuary to pray, he will not
prevail.
¹³ This is the word that the Lord spoke
concerning Moab in the past. ¹⁴ But now the
Lord has spoken, saying, "In three years, like
the years of a hired worker, the glory of Moab
will be brought into contempt, in spite of all
his great multitude, and those who remain
will be very few and feeble."

*1. How would you summarize this oracle,
  spoken against Moab?*

2. Why is 15:5 surprising, given the nature of the oracle and what we've read up to this point?

3. What is the connection between 15:5 and 16:5?

PONDER God's judgement can be both necessary and right, yet also lamentable. What is your attitude towards it?

PRAYER IDEAS Ask God to give you a heart that "cries out" for those who are under his judgement (15:5). Thank him for providing the one who sits on the throne "established in steadfast love" (16:5).

POINTERS 15:1: The word 'oracle' means 'word', 'utterance' or 'burden'.
15:1: Moab lay to the east of Judah.

READING 26   ISAIAH 17

An oracle concerning Damascus.

Behold, Damascus will cease to be a city
  and will become a heap of ruins.
² The cities of Aroer are deserted;
  they will be for flocks,
  which will lie down, and none will make
    them afraid.
³ The fortress will disappear from Ephraim,
  and the kingdom from Damascus;
and the remnant of Syria will be
  like the glory of the children of Israel,
  declares the LORD of hosts.

⁴ And in that day the glory of Jacob will be
    brought low,
  and the fat of his flesh will grow lean.
⁵ And it shall be as when the reaper gathers
    standing grain
  and his arm harvests the ears,
and as when one gleans the ears of grain
  in the Valley of Rephaim.
⁶ Gleanings will be left in it,
  as when an olive tree is beaten—
two or three berries
  in the top of the highest bough,
four or five
  on the branches of a fruit tree,
  declares the LORD God of Israel.

⁷ In that day man will look to his Maker, and his eyes will look on the Holy One of Israel. ⁸ He will not look to the altars, the work of his hands, and he will not look on what his own fingers have made, either the Asherim or the altars of incense.

⁹ In that day their strong cities will be like the deserted places of the wooded heights and the hilltops, which they deserted because of the children of Israel, and there will be desolation.

¹⁰ For you have forgotten the God of your
    salvation
  and have not remembered the Rock of
    your refuge;
therefore, though you plant pleasant
    plants
  and sow the vine-branch of a stranger,
¹¹ though you make them grow on the day
    that you plant them,
  and make them blossom in the morning
    that you sow,
yet the harvest will flee away
  in a day of grief and incurable pain.

¹² Ah, the thunder of many peoples;
  they thunder like the thundering of the
    sea!

Ah, the roar of nations;
     they roar like the roaring of mighty
          waters!
¹³ The nations roar like the roaring of many
          waters,
     but he will rebuke them, and they will
          flee far away,
chased like chaff on the mountains before
          the wind
     and whirling dust before the storm.
¹⁴ At evening time, behold, terror!
     Before morning, they are no more!
This is the portion of those who loot us,
     and the lot of those who plunder us.

1. What will happen to Damascus in verses
   1-3? What will happen to Jacob in verses
   4-6?

2. Why will this happen to Damascus (v. 8)?

3. What impact will this have upon these
   two nations (vv. 7-11)?

PONDER Do you find man's response to
God's judgement in verses 7-9 surprising?
How do these verses compare to your
response to God's judgement?

PRAYER IDEAS Ask God to drive people to
trust only in him because of the past and
future judgements he has revealed in his word.

POINTER v. 1: Damascus was the capital of
Syria. It lay to the north of Judah.

READING 27   ISAIAH 18

Ah, land of whirring wings
     that is beyond the rivers of Cush,
² which sends ambassadors by the sea,
     in vessels of papyrus on the waters!
Go, you swift messengers,
     to a nation, tall and smooth,
to a people feared near and far,
     a nation mighty and conquering,
     whose land the rivers divide.

³ All you inhabitants of the world,
     you who dwell on the earth,
when a signal is raised on the mountains,
          look!
     When a trumpet is blown, hear!
⁴ For thus the LORD said to me:
"I will quietly look from my dwelling
     like clear heat in sunshine,
     like a cloud of dew in the heat of
          harvest."

⁵ For before the harvest, when the blossom
          is over,
     and the flower becomes a ripening
          grape,
he cuts off the shoots with pruning hooks,
     and the spreading branches he lops off
          and clears away.
⁶ They shall all of them be left
     to the birds of prey of the mountains
     and to the beasts of the earth.
And the birds of prey will summer on them,
     and all the beasts of the earth will
          winter on them.

⁷ At that time tribute will be brought to the
LORD of hosts

     from a people tall and smooth,
          from a people feared near and far,
     a nation mighty and conquering,

whose land the rivers divide,

to Mount Zion, the place of the name of the LORD of hosts.

This chapter appears to be a speech delivered to the ambassadors of Cush—a speech that they were to take back to their leaders (v. 2).

1. *What diplomatic, political and military activities do the people of Cush appear to be involved in?*

2. *What is God's response in verses 4-5?*

3. *While this prophecy may not have ever reached Cush, it was certainly heard by King Hezekiah and the kingdom of Judah. What message should they have taken from it?*

PONDER God is sovereign over all diplomatic, political and military endeavours. Where do you see his sovereignty at work in your life?

PRAYER IDEAS Ask God to help the leaders of your community, your state and your nation to govern wisely and well. Ask him to help them trust in Jesus.

POINTER v. 1: Cush was the large region of the fourth cataract of the Nile, embracing modern Sudan, Ethiopia and Somaliland. It lay to the south of Judah.

READING 28   ISAIAH 19:1-15

An oracle concerning Egypt.

Behold, the LORD is riding on a swift cloud
    and comes to Egypt;
and the idols of Egypt will tremble at his
        presence,
    and the heart of the Egyptians will melt
        within them.
2 And I will stir up Egyptians against
        Egyptians,
and they will fight, each against another
and each against his neighbor,
city against city, kingdom against
        kingdom;
3 and the spirit of the Egyptians within them
        will be emptied out,
    and I will confound their counsel;
and they will inquire of the idols and the
        sorcerers,

and the mediums and the necromancers;
4 and I will give over the Egyptians
    into the hand of a hard master,
and a fierce king will rule over them,
    declares the Lord GOD of hosts.

5 And the waters of the sea will be dried up,
    and the river will be dry and parched,
6 and its canals will become foul,
    and the branches of Egypt's Nile will
        diminish and dry up,
    reeds and rushes will rot away.
7 There will be bare places by the Nile,
    on the brink of the Nile,
and all that is sown by the Nile will be
        parched,
    will be driven away, and will be no more.
8 The fishermen will mourn and lament,
    all who cast a hook in the Nile;

and they will languish
   who spread nets on the water.
⁹ The workers in combed flax will be in
     despair,
   and the weavers of white cotton.
¹⁰ Those who are the pillars of the land will
     be crushed,
   and all who work for pay will be grieved.

¹¹ The princes of Zoan are utterly foolish;
   the wisest counselors of Pharaoh give
     stupid counsel.
How can you say to Pharaoh,
   "I am a son of the wise,
   a son of ancient kings"?
¹² Where then are your wise men?
   Let them tell you
   that they might know what the LORD
     of hosts has purposed against
     Egypt.
¹³ The princes of Zoan have become fools,
   and the princes of Memphis are
     deluded;
those who are the cornerstones of her tribes
   have made Egypt stagger.
¹⁴ The LORD has mingled within her a spirit of
     confusion,
and they will make Egypt stagger in all its
     deeds,
   as a drunken man staggers in his vomit.

¹⁵ And there will be nothing for Egypt
   that head or tail, palm branch or reed,
     may do.

1. What do the Egyptians put their trust in?

2. What does God do with these things?

*3. How do you think an Israelite would have
responded to this passage?*

PONDER What do you place your trust in?
Are they the same sorts of things that the
Egyptians put their trust in?

PRAYER IDEAS Thank God for giving us his
Son Jesus, Jesus' death and Jesus' resurrection
as the only sure things we can trust.

POINTER v. 1: Egypt lay to the south of
Judah.

READING 29   ISAIAH 19:16-25

In that day the Egyptians will be like women,
and tremble with fear before the hand that
the LORD of hosts shakes over them. ¹⁷ And
the land of Judah will become a terror to the
Egyptians. Everyone to whom it is mentioned
will fear because of the purpose that the LORD
of hosts has purposed against them.
  ¹⁸ In that day there will be five cities in
the land of Egypt that speak the language of
Canaan and swear allegiance to the LORD of
hosts. One of these will be called the City of
Destruction.

¹⁹ In that day there will be an altar to the
LORD in the midst of the land of Egypt, and
a pillar to the LORD at its border. ²⁰ It will be
a sign and a witness to the LORD of hosts in
the land of Egypt. When they cry to the LORD
because of oppressors, he will send them
a savior and defender, and deliver them.
²¹ And the LORD will make himself known to
the Egyptians, and the Egyptians will know
the LORD in that day and worship with sacrifice
and offering, and they will make vows to the
LORD and perform them. ²² And the LORD will

strike Egypt, striking and healing, and they will return to the Lord, and he will listen to their pleas for mercy and heal them.

²³ In that day there will be a highway from Egypt to Assyria, and Assyria will come into Egypt, and Egypt into Assyria, and the Egyptians will worship with the Assyrians.

²⁴ In that day Israel will be the third with Egypt and Assyria, a blessing in the midst of the earth, ²⁵ whom the Lord of hosts has blessed, saying, "Blessed be Egypt my people, and Assyria the work of my hands, and Israel my inheritance."

1. How will God reverse the roles of Egypt and Judah?

2. How is salvation depicted in these verses?

3. How does the prophecy in this passage fulfil God's promise to Abraham in Genesis 12:3?²⁶

PONDER How is God's promise to Abraham ultimately fulfilled in Revelation 7:9-12?²⁷

PRAYER IDEAS Thank God for the heaven he has promised in which people from every tribe, nation and tongue will sing the praises of Jesus. Ask him to help you live your life in light of this promise.

READING 30   ISAIAH 20

In the year that the commander in chief, who was sent by Sargon the king of Assyria, came to Ashdod and fought against it and captured it— ² at that time the Lord spoke by Isaiah the son of Amoz, saying, "Go, and loose the sackcloth from your waist and take off your sandals from your feet," and he did so, walking naked and barefoot.

³ Then the Lord said, "As my servant Isaiah has walked naked and barefoot for three years as a sign and a portent against Egypt and Cush, ⁴ so shall the king of Assyria lead away the Egyptian captives and the Cushite exiles, both the young and the old, naked and barefoot, with buttocks uncovered, the nakedness of Egypt. ⁵ Then they shall be

dismayed and ashamed because of Cush their hope and of Egypt their boast. ⁶ And the inhabitants of this coastland will say in that day, 'Behold, this is what has happened to those in whom we hoped and to whom we fled for help to be delivered from the king of Assyria! And we, how shall we escape?'"

1. How does God humble Egypt and Cush?

2. What is the response from the inhabitants of the coastlands?

---

26. "I will bless those who bless you, and him who dishonors you I will curse, and in you all the families of the earth shall be blessed."

27. After this I looked, and behold, a great multitude that no one could number, from every nation, from all tribes and peoples and languages, standing before the throne and before the Lamb, clothed in white robes, with palm branches in their hands, ¹⁰ and crying out with a loud voice, "Salvation belongs to our God who sits on the throne, and to the Lamb!" ¹¹ And all the angels were standing around the throne and around the elders and the four living creatures, and they fell on their faces before the throne and worshiped God, ¹² saying, "Amen! Blessing and glory and wisdom and thanksgiving and honor and power and might be to our God forever and ever! Amen."

PONDER Judah has looked to the south, east, west and north. Which nation can Judah trust? Who must Judah trust instead?

PRAYER IDEAS Thank God for the folly of the cross. Thank God for humbling the proud and using the weak things of the world to shame the strong.

READING 31   ISAIAH 21:1-10

The oracle concerning the wilderness of the sea.

As whirlwinds in the Negeb sweep on,
    it comes from the wilderness,
    from a terrible land.
² A stern vision is told to me;
    the traitor betrays,
    and the destroyer destroys.
Go up, O Elam;
    lay siege, O Media;
all the sighing she has caused
    I bring to an end.
³ Therefore my loins are filled with anguish;
    pangs have seized me,
    like the pangs of a woman in labor;
I am bowed down so that I cannot hear;
    I am dismayed so that I cannot see.
⁴ My heart staggers; horror has appalled me;
    the twilight I longed for
    has been turned for me into trembling.
⁵ They prepare the table,
    they spread the rugs,
    they eat, they drink.
Arise, O princes;
    oil the shield!
⁶ For thus the Lord said to me:
"Go, set a watchman;
    let him announce what he sees.
⁷ When he sees riders, horsemen in pairs,
    riders on donkeys, riders on camels,
let him listen diligently,
    very diligently."
⁸ Then he who saw cried out:
"Upon a watchtower I stand, O Lᴏʀᴅ,
    continually by day,
and at my post I am stationed
    whole nights.

⁹ And behold, here come riders,
    horsemen in pairs!"
And he answered,
    "Fallen, fallen is Babylon;
and all the carved images of her gods
    he has shattered to the ground."
¹⁰ O my threshed and winnowed one,
    what I have heard from the Lᴏʀᴅ of
        hosts,
    the God of Israel, I announce to you.

1. What does the watchman see?

2. What does this oracle have to say about Babylon (v. 9)?

3. If Babylon is undergoing a political ascent, what is the temptation that faces Judah?

PONDER When are you tempted to put your trust in world powers? Why is it futile to do so?

PRAYER IDEAS Thank God for giving you a hope and a future that does not lie in the world powers of our day and age, but in God's eternal kingdom, established by his Son Jesus.

POINTER v. 2: 'Elam' refers to Persia.

The oracle concerning Dumah.

One is calling to me from Seir,
    "Watchman, what time of the night?
    Watchman, what time of the night?"
12 The watchman says:
"Morning comes, and also the night.
    If you will inquire, inquire;
    come back again."

13 The oracle concerning Arabia.

In the thickets in Arabia you will lodge,
    O caravans of Dedanites.
14 To the thirsty bring water;
    meet the fugitive with bread,
    O inhabitants of the land of Tema.
15 For they have fled from the swords,
    from the drawn sword,
from the bent bow,
    and from the press of battle.

16 For thus the Lord said to me, "Within a year, according to the years of a hired worker, all the glory of Kedar will come to an end. 17 And the remainder of the archers of the mighty men of the sons of Kedar will be few, for the LORD, the God of Israel, has spoken."

1. Who seems to be the watchman in this passage?

2. What does he say about the fate of those who have allied themselves with Babylon? (Hint: see pointers for verses 11, 13 and 14.)

PONDER Who is presented as being in control of the fate of all nations?

PRAYER IDEAS Thank God that his word is trustworthy and reliable—both his promises to bless and his promises to judge.

POINTERS v. 11: 'Seir' refers to Edom, which lay to the south of Judah.
    vv. 11, 13, 14: Dumah, Dedan and Tema lay to the north of Judah in the Arabian desert region between Judah and Babylon. It is likely that Babylonian emissaries passed through this region to avoid travelling through Assyria. (In all likelihood, they sought to recruit their assistance against Assyria.)
    v. 17: 'Kedar' was a collective term for the desert tribes in general.

The oracle concerning the valley of vision.

What do you mean that you have gone up,
    all of you, to the housetops,
2 you who are full of shoutings,
    tumultuous city, exultant town?
Your slain are not slain with the sword
    or dead in battle.
3 All your leaders have fled together;
    without the bow they were captured.

All of you who were found were captured,
    though they had fled far away.
4 Therefore I said:
"Look away from me;
    let me weep bitter tears;
do not labor to comfort me
    concerning the destruction of the
        daughter of my people."

5 For the Lord GOD of hosts has a day

of tumult and trampling and confusion
   in the valley of vision,
a battering down of walls
   and a shouting to the mountains.
⁶ And Elam bore the quiver
   with chariots and horsemen,
   and Kir uncovered the shield.
⁷ Your choicest valleys were full of chariots,
   and the horsemen took their stand at
      the gates.
⁸ He has taken away the covering of Judah.

   In that day you looked to the weapons of
the House of the Forest, ⁹ and you saw that
the breaches of the city of David were many.
You collected the waters of the lower pool,
¹⁰ and you counted the houses of Jerusalem,
and you broke down the houses to fortify
the wall. ¹¹ You made a reservoir between the
two walls for the water of the old pool. But
you did not look to him who did it, or see him
who planned it long ago.

¹² In that day the Lord GOD of hosts
   called for weeping and mourning,
   for baldness and wearing sackcloth;
¹³ and behold, joy and gladness,
   killing oxen and slaughtering sheep,
   eating flesh and drinking wine.
"Let us eat and drink,
   for tomorrow we die."
¹⁴ The LORD of hosts has revealed himself in
      my ears:
"Surely this iniquity will not be atoned for
      you until you die,"
says the Lord GOD of hosts.

¹⁵ Thus says the Lord GOD of hosts, "Come,
go to this steward, to Shebna, who is over the
household, and say to him: ¹⁶ What have you
to do here, and whom have you here, that
you have cut out here a tomb for yourself,
you who cut out a tomb on the height and

carve a dwelling for yourself in the rock?
¹⁷ Behold, the LORD will hurl you away
violently, O you strong man. He will seize
firm hold on you ¹⁸ and whirl you around and
around, and throw you like a ball into a wide
land. There you shall die, and there shall be
your glorious chariots, you shame of your
master's house. ¹⁹ I will thrust you from your
office, and you will be pulled down from your
station. ²⁰ In that day I will call my servant
Eliakim the son of Hilkiah, ²¹ and I will clothe
him with your robe, and will bind your sash
on him, and will commit your authority to
his hand. And he shall be a father to the
inhabitants of Jerusalem and to the house
of Judah. ²² And I will place on his shoulder
the key of the house of David. He shall open,
and none shall shut; and he shall shut, and
none shall open. ²³ And I will fasten him like
a peg in a secure place, and he will become a
throne of honor to his father's house. ²⁴ And
they will hang on him the whole honor of his
father's house, the offspring and issue, every
small vessel, from the cups to all the flagons.
²⁵ In that day, declares the LORD of hosts, the
peg that was fastened in a secure place will
give way, and it will be cut down and fall, and
the load that was on it will be cut off, for the
LORD has spoken."

*1. What is the word to Judah's populace in
general (vv. 1-14)?*

*2. What is the word to Shebna in particular
(vv. 15-25; cf. 36:3²⁸)?*

---

28. And there came out to him Eliakim the son of Hilkiah, who
was over the household, and Shebna the secretary, and Joah the
son of Asaph, the recorder.

3. How will Eliakim be different to Shebna?

PRAYER IDEAS Thank God for the godly leaders you know. Ask him to sustain and uphold them, and to continue raising up more godly leaders.

PONDER What is the impact of a godly leader on the people he leads? What is the impact of an ungodly leader on the people he leads?

POINTERS v. 6: 'Elam' refers to Persia.
v. 6: Kir was located in Moab.

READING 34   ISAIAH 23

The oracle concerning Tyre.

Wail, O ships of Tarshish,
    for Tyre is laid waste, without house or
        harbor!
From the land of Cyprus
    it is revealed to them.
² Be still, O inhabitants of the coast;
    the merchants of Sidon, who cross the
        sea, have filled you.
³ And on many waters
your revenue was the grain of Shihor,
    the harvest of the Nile;
    you were the merchant of the nations.
⁴ Be ashamed, O Sidon, for the sea has
        spoken,
    the stronghold of the sea, saying:
"I have neither labored nor given birth,
    I have neither reared young men
    nor brought up young women."
⁵ When the report comes to Egypt,
    they will be in anguish over the report
        about Tyre.
⁶ Cross over to Tarshish;
    wail, O inhabitants of the coast!
⁷ Is this your exultant city
    whose origin is from days of old,
whose feet carried her
    to settle far away?
⁸ Who has purposed this
    against Tyre, the bestower of crowns,
whose merchants were princes,
    whose traders were the honored of

the earth?
⁹ The LORD of hosts has purposed it,
    to defile the pompous pride of all glory,
    to dishonor all the honored of the earth.
¹⁰ Cross over your land like the Nile,
    O daughter of Tarshish;
    there is no restraint anymore.
¹¹ He has stretched out his hand over the
        sea;
he has shaken the kingdoms;
the LORD has given command concerning
        Canaan
    to destroy its strongholds.
¹² And he said:
"You will no more exult,
    O oppressed virgin daughter of Sidon;
arise, cross over to Cyprus,
    even there you will have no rest."

¹³ Behold the land of the Chaldeans! This is the people that was not; Assyria destined it for wild beasts. They erected their siege towers, they stripped her palaces bare, they made her a ruin.

¹⁴ Wail, O ships of Tarshish,
    for your stronghold is laid waste.

¹⁵ In that day Tyre will be forgotten for seventy years, like the days of one king. At the end of seventy years, it will happen to Tyre as in the song of the prostitute:

¹⁶ "Take a harp;
    go about the city,
    O forgotten prostitute!
Make sweet melody;
    sing many songs,
    that you may be remembered."

¹⁷ At the end of seventy years, the LORD will visit Tyre, and she will return to her wages and will prostitute herself with all the kingdoms of the world on the face of the earth. ¹⁸ Her merchandise and her wages will be holy to the LORD. It will not be stored or hoarded, but her merchandise will supply abundant food and fine clothing for those who dwell before the LORD.

1. Describe the fate of Tyre.

2. What is the connection that verse 13 draws between Tyre and Babylon (i.e. the "land of the Chaldeans")?

3. What is the reason for Tyre's downfall at God's hand?

PONDER Read Proverbs 30:7-9.²⁹ What is the connection between wealth and pride, and what we desire?

PRAYER IDEAS Thank God for Jesus—that though he was rich, he became poor for our sakes (2 Cor 8:9³⁰). Ask God to help you view yourself rightly (cf. Jas 1:9-11³¹).

POINTERS v. 1: Tyre was proverbial for its commercial wealth. It was the principal seaport on the Phoenician coast.
    v. 1: Tarshish was a mineral-rich land in the western Mediterranean, linked with Tartessus in Spain. It was also a far-flung Phoenician colony.
    v. 2: Sidon, along with Tyre, was a leading Phoenician city.

READING 35   ISAIAH 24

Behold, the LORD will empty the earth and make it desolate,
    and he will twist its surface and scatter its inhabitants.
² And it shall be, as with the people, so with the priest;
    as with the slave, so with his master;
    as with the maid, so with her mistress;
as with the buyer, so with the seller;
    as with the lender, so with the borrower;

---

29. Two things I ask of you;
    deny them not to me before I die:
  ⁸ Remove far from me falsehood and lying;
    give me neither poverty nor riches;
    feed me with the food that is needful for me,
  ⁹ lest I be full and deny you
    and say, "Who is the LORD?"
or lest I be poor and steal
    and profane the name of my God.

30. For you know the grace of our Lord Jesus Christ, that though he was rich, yet for your sake he became poor, so that you by his poverty might become rich.
31. Let the lowly brother boast in his exaltation, ¹⁰ and the rich in his humiliation, because like a flower of the grass he will pass away. ¹¹ For the sun rises with its scorching heat and withers the grass; its flower falls, and its beauty perishes. So also will the rich man fade away in the midst of his pursuits.

as with the creditor, so with the debtor.
³ The earth shall be utterly empty and
    utterly plundered;
    for the Lord has spoken this word.

⁴ The earth mourns and withers;
    the world languishes and withers;
    the highest people of the earth languish.
⁵ The earth lies defiled
    under its inhabitants;
for they have transgressed the laws,
    violated the statutes,
    broken the everlasting covenant.
⁶ Therefore a curse devours the earth,
    and its inhabitants suffer for their guilt;
therefore the inhabitants of the earth are
    scorched,
    and few men are left.
⁷ The wine mourns,
    the vine languishes,
    all the merry-hearted sigh.
⁸ The mirth of the tambourines is stilled,
    the noise of the jubilant has ceased,
    the mirth of the lyre is stilled.
⁹ No more do they drink wine with singing;
    strong drink is bitter to those who drink
    it.
¹⁰ The wasted city is broken down;
    every house is shut up so that none can
    enter.
¹¹ There is an outcry in the streets for lack
    of wine;
    all joy has grown dark;
    the gladness of the earth is banished.
¹² Desolation is left in the city;
    the gates are battered into ruins.
¹³ For thus it shall be in the midst of the
    earth
    among the nations,
as when an olive tree is beaten,
    as at the gleaning when the grape
    harvest is done.

¹⁴ They lift up their voices, they sing for joy;
    over the majesty of the Lord they shout
    from the west.

¹⁵ Therefore in the east give glory to the
    Lord;
    in the coastlands of the sea, give glory
    to the name of the Lord, the God
    of Israel.
¹⁶ From the ends of the earth we hear songs
    of praise,
    of glory to the Righteous One.
But I say, "I waste away,
    I waste away. Woe is me!
For the traitors have betrayed,
    with betrayal the traitors have
    betrayed."

¹⁷ Terror and the pit and the snare
    are upon you, O inhabitant of the earth!
¹⁸ He who flees at the sound of the terror
    shall fall into the pit,
and he who climbs out of the pit
    shall be caught in the snare.
For the windows of heaven are opened,
    and the foundations of the earth
    tremble.
¹⁹ The earth is utterly broken,
    the earth is split apart,
    the earth is violently shaken.
²⁰ The earth staggers like a drunken man;
    it sways like a hut;
its transgression lies heavy upon it,
    and it falls, and will not rise again.

²¹ On that day the Lord will punish
    the host of heaven, in heaven,
    and the kings of the earth, on the
    earth.
²² They will be gathered together
    as prisoners in a pit;
they will be shut up in a prison,
    and after many days they will be
    punished.
²³ Then the moon will be confounded
    and the sun ashamed,
for the Lord of hosts reigns
    on Mount Zion and in Jerusalem,
and his glory will be before his elders.

1. Where does the terror lie in this vision?

2. Where does the glory lie in this vision?

3. How does Isaiah hold both glory and

terror together in his depiction of judgement?

PONDER How was the cross part of God's judgement? How did it display his glory?

PRAYER IDEAS Thank God for his judgement on Jesus at the cross. Ask him to help you to grasp why this is both glorious and terrifying.

READING 36   ISAIAH 25

O LORD, you are my God;
I will exalt you; I will praise your name,
for you have done wonderful things,
    plans formed of old, faithful and sure.
² For you have made the city a heap,
    the fortified city a ruin;
the foreigners' palace is a city no more;
    it will never be rebuilt.
³ Therefore strong peoples will glorify you;
    cities of ruthless nations will fear you.
⁴ For you have been a stronghold to the
        poor,
    a stronghold to the needy in his distress,
a shelter from the storm and a shade from
        the heat;
    for the breath of the ruthless is like a
        storm against a wall,
⁵ like heat in a dry place.
    You subdue the noise of the foreigners;
as heat by the shade of a cloud,
    so the song of the ruthless is put down.

⁶ On this mountain the LORD of hosts will
        make for all peoples
    a feast of rich food, a feast of well-aged
        wine,
    of rich food full of marrow, of aged
        wine well refined.
⁷ And he will swallow up on this mountain
    the covering that is cast over all peoples,

the veil that is spread over all nations.
    ⁸ He will swallow up death forever;
and the Lord GOD will wipe away tears from
        all faces,
    and the reproach of his people he will
        take away from all the earth,
    for the LORD has spoken.
⁹ It will be said on that day,
    "Behold, this is our God; we have waited
        for him, that he might save us.
    This is the LORD; we have waited for him;
    let us be glad and rejoice in his
        salvation."
¹⁰ For the hand of the LORD will rest on this
        mountain,
    and Moab shall be trampled down in his
        place,
    as straw is trampled down in a dunghill.
¹¹ And he will spread out his hands in the
        midst of it
    as a swimmer spreads his hands out to
        swim,
    but the LORD will lay low his pompous
        pride together with the skill of
        his hands.
¹² And the high fortifications of his walls he
        will bring down,
    lay low, and cast to the ground, to the
        dust.

1. *What is God being praised for here?*

PONDER Read Revelation 21:1-8.[32] What is the fate of God's people? What is the fate of sinners?

PRAYER IDEAS Thank God for his judgement and his victory over your enemies—Satan, sin and death—in the cross of Christ. Ask him to hasten the day when his victory will be realized in full.

2. *What indicators are there that this chapter speaks of the eschatological (i.e. end times) victory of God?*

READING 37   ISAIAH 26:1-11

In that day this song will be sung in the land of Judah:

"We have a strong city;
    he sets up salvation
    as walls and bulwarks.
2 Open the gates,
    that the righteous nation that keeps
        faith may enter in.
3 You keep him in perfect peace
    whose mind is stayed on you,
    because he trusts in you.
4 Trust in the Lord forever,
    for the Lord God is an everlasting rock.
5 For he has humbled
    the inhabitants of the height,
    the lofty city.
He lays it low, lays it low to the ground,
    casts it to the dust.
6 The foot tramples it,
    the feet of the poor,
    the steps of the needy."

7 The path of the righteous is level;
    you make level the way of the righteous.
8 In the path of your judgments,
    O Lord, we wait for you;
your name and remembrance
    are the desire of our soul.
9 My soul yearns for you in the night;
    my spirit within me earnestly seeks you.
For when your judgments are in the earth,
    the inhabitants of the world learn
        righteousness.
10 If favor is shown to the wicked,
    he does not learn righteousness;
in the land of uprightness he deals corruptly
    and does not see the majesty of the
        Lord.
11 O Lord, your hand is lifted up,
    but they do not see it.
Let them see your zeal for your people, and
        be ashamed.
    Let the fire for your adversaries
        consume them.

---

32. Then I saw a new heaven and a new earth, for the first heaven and the first earth had passed away, and the sea was no more. 2 And I saw the holy city, new Jerusalem, coming down out of heaven from God, prepared as a bride adorned for her husband. 3 And I heard a loud voice from the throne saying, "Behold, the dwelling place of God is with man. He will dwell with them, and they will be his people, and God himself will be with them as their God. 4 He will wipe away every tear from their eyes, and death shall be no more, neither shall there be mourning, nor crying, nor pain anymore, for the former things have passed away."

5 And he who was seated on the throne said, "Behold, I am making all things new." Also he said, "Write this down, for these words are trustworthy and true." 6 And he said to me, "It is done! I am the Alpha and the Omega, the beginning and the end. To the thirsty I will give from the spring of the water of life without payment. 7 The one who conquers will have this heritage, and I will be his God and he will be my son. 8 But as for the cowardly, the faithless, the detestable, as for murderers, the sexually immoral, sorcerers, idolaters, and all liars, their portion will be in the lake that burns with fire and sulfur, which is the second death."

1. Compare and contrast the strong city in verses 1-2 (God's new Zion) and the lofty city in verse 5 (the human city; cf. 24:10,[33] 25:2[34]). What are the similarities? What are the differences?

2. What is so good about righteousness (vv. 8-11)?

3. Why does the singer of this song desire the Lord? Do you desire him in the same way?

PONDER What should be your attitude as you wait for the Lord's return (cf. 2 Pet 3:8-13[35])?

PRAYER IDEAS Ask God to help you to be patient as you wait for his return.

READING 38   ISAIAH 26:12-21

O LORD, you will ordain peace for us,
for you have indeed done for us all our works.
¹³ O LORD our God,
other lords besides you have ruled over us,
but your name alone we bring to remembrance.
¹⁴ They are dead, they will not live;
they are shades, they will not arise;
to that end you have visited them with destruction
and wiped out all remembrance of them.
¹⁵ But you have increased the nation, O LORD,
you have increased the nation; you are glorified;
you have enlarged all the borders of the land.

¹⁶ O LORD, in distress they sought you;
they poured out a whispered prayer
when your discipline was upon them.
¹⁷ Like a pregnant woman
who writhes and cries out in her pangs
when she is near to giving birth,
so were we because of you, O LORD;
¹⁸ we were pregnant, we writhed,
but we have given birth to wind.
We have accomplished no deliverance in the earth,
and the inhabitants of the world have not fallen.
¹⁹ Your dead shall live; their bodies shall rise.
You who dwell in the dust, awake and sing for joy!
For your dew is a dew of light,
and the earth will give birth to the dead.

---

33. The wasted city is broken down;
every house is shut up so that none can enter.
34. For you have made the city a heap,
the fortified city a ruin;
the foreigners' palace is a city no more;
it will never be rebuilt.
35. But do not overlook this one fact, beloved, that with the Lord one day is as a thousand years, and a thousand years as one day. ⁹ The Lord is not slow to fulfill his promise as some count slowness, but is patient toward you, not wishing that any should perish, but that all should reach repentance. ¹⁰ But the

day of the Lord will come like a thief, and then the heavens will pass away with a roar, and the heavenly bodies will be burned up and dissolved, and the earth and the works that are done on it will be exposed.
¹¹ Since all these things are thus to be dissolved, what sort of people ought you to be in lives of holiness and godliness, ¹² waiting for and hastening the coming of the day of God, because of which the heavens will be set on fire and dissolved, and the heavenly bodies will melt as they burn! ¹³ But according to his promise we are waiting for new heavens and a new earth in which righteousness dwells.

20 Come, my people, enter your chambers,
        and shut your doors behind you;
hide yourselves for a little while
        until the fury has passed by.
21 For behold, the LORD is coming out from
                his place
        to punish the inhabitants of the earth
                for their iniquity,
and the earth will disclose the blood shed
                on it,
        and will no more cover its slain.

1. How does God deal with those who are
   waiting for him? Does this treatment seem
   fair to you?

2. What effect does this treatment have on
   those who are waiting?

3. Death is the great enemy of those who
   are waiting. What is the solution to this
   problem (v. 19)?

PONDER Read 1 Corinthians 15:20-26.[36] How
does Jesus' resurrection give you hope as you
wait for him patiently?

PRAYER IDEAS Thank God for his promise to
resurrect those who trust in his resurrected Son.

READING 39   ISAIAH 27:1-6

In that day the LORD with his hard and great
and strong sword will punish Leviathan
the fleeing serpent, Leviathan the twisting
serpent, and he will slay the dragon that is in
the sea.

2 In that day,
"A pleasant vineyard, sing of it!
        3 I, the LORD, am its keeper;
        every moment I water it.
        Lest anyone punish it,
I keep it night and day;
        4 I have no wrath.
Would that I had thorns and briers to battle!
        I would march against them,
        I would burn them up together.
5 Or let them lay hold of my protection,
        let them make peace with me,
        let them make peace with me."

6 In days to come Jacob shall take root,
        Israel shall blossom and put forth shoots
        and fill the whole world with fruit.

1. How would you describe this song which
   God sings to his people (vv. 3-6)?

2. How is this song a reversal of Isaiah 5:1-7
   (see the appendix, p. 70)?

---

36. But in fact Christ has been raised from the dead, the
firstfruits of those who have fallen asleep. 21 For as by a man
came death, by a man has come also the resurrection of the
dead. 22 For as in Adam all die, so also in Christ shall all be
made alive. 23 But each in his own order: Christ the firstfruits,
then at his coming those who belong to Christ. 24 Then comes
the end, when he delivers the kingdom to God the Father after
destroying every rule and every authority and power. 25 For he
must reign until he has put all his enemies under his feet. 26 The
last enemy to be destroyed is death.

PONDER How has your heavenly Father been good to you?

PRAYER IDEAS Thank God for loving you and taking care of you.

READING 40   ISAIAH 27:7-13

Has he struck them as he struck those who struck them?
Or have they been slain as their slayers were slain?
⁸ Measure by measure, by exile you contended with them;
he removed them with his fierce breath in the day of the east wind.
⁹ Therefore by this the guilt of Jacob will be atoned for,
and this will be the full fruit of the removal of his sin:
when he makes all the stones of the altars like chalkstones crushed to pieces,
no Asherim or incense altars will remain standing.
¹⁰ For the fortified city is solitary,
a habitation deserted and forsaken, like the wilderness;
there the calf grazes;
there it lies down and strips its branches.
¹¹ When its boughs are dry, they are broken;
women come and make a fire of them.
For this is a people without discernment;
therefore he who made them will not have compassion on them;
he who formed them will show them no favor.

¹² In that day from the river Euphrates to the Brook of Egypt the LORD will thresh out the grain, and you will be gleaned one by one, O people of Israel. ¹³ And in that day a great trumpet will be blown, and those who were lost in the land of Assyria and those who were driven out to the land of Egypt will come and worship the LORD on the holy mountain at Jerusalem.

1. After the idyllic picture of verses 3-6, verses 7-11 mark an abrupt return to the present waiting period. How does God cleanse his people in these verses?

2. What is terrifying about verses 12-13? What is comforting about these verses?

PONDER God continues to cleanse and refine his people (cf. 1 Pet 1:7³⁷). Where have you seen him at work in your life recently?

PRAYER IDEAS Ask God to refine and sustain you during this time as you wait for his return.

---

37. ... so that the tested genuineness of your faith—more precious than gold that perishes though it is tested by fire—may be found to result in praise and glory and honor at the revelation of Jesus Christ.

THE TEN COMMANDMENTS

INTRODUCTION

Everyone has heard of the Ten Commandments. But how many of them could you list? Do they even matter anyway? This set of studies helps us to see how the commandments provide a concise guide to how to live in proper relationship with God and with other people.

You might like to use this prayer (or your own variation of it) before each of the next 20 studies:

Dear Father,
Thank you for opening the door for me to relationship with you through Jesus. Help me to relate to you and to everyone I meet properly. For the sake of your Son,
Amen

| READING 41 | EXODUS 19:1-6, 19:16-20:21 | ◼ |

Exodus 19:1-6

On the third new moon after the people of Israel had gone out of the land of Egypt, on that day they came into the wilderness of Sinai. ² They set out from Rephidim and came into the wilderness of Sinai, and they encamped in the wilderness. There Israel encamped before the mountain, ³ while Moses went up to God. The LORD called to him out of the mountain, saying, "Thus you shall say to the house of Jacob, and tell the people of Israel: ⁴ You yourselves have seen what I did to the Egyptians, and how I bore you on eagles' wings and brought you to myself. ⁵ Now therefore, if you will indeed obey my voice and keep my covenant, you shall be my treasured possession among all peoples, for all the earth is mine; ⁶ and you shall be to me a kingdom of priests and a holy nation. These are the words that you shall speak to the people of Israel."

Exodus 19:16-20:21

On the morning of the third day there were thunders and lightnings and a thick cloud on the mountain and a very loud trumpet blast, so that all the people in the camp trembled. ¹⁷ Then Moses brought the people out of the camp to meet God, and they took their stand at the foot of the mountain. ¹⁸ Now Mount Sinai was wrapped in smoke because the LORD had descended on it in fire. The smoke of it went up like the smoke of a kiln, and the whole mountain trembled greatly. ¹⁹ And as the sound of the trumpet grew louder and louder, Moses spoke, and God answered him in thunder. ²⁰ The LORD came down on Mount Sinai, to the top of the mountain. And the LORD called Moses to the top of the mountain, and Moses went up.
²¹ And the LORD said to Moses, "Go down and warn the people, lest they break through to the LORD to look and many of them perish. ²² Also let the priests who come near to the

Lord consecrate themselves, lest the Lord break out against them." 23 And Moses said to the Lord, "The people cannot come up to Mount Sinai, for you yourself warned us, saying, 'Set limits around the mountain and consecrate it.'" 24 And the Lord said to him, "Go down, and come up bringing Aaron with you. But do not let the priests and the people break through to come up to the Lord, lest he break out against them." 25 So Moses went down to the people and told them.

20:1 And God spoke all these words, saying, 2 "I am the Lord your God, who brought you out of the land of Egypt, out of the house of slavery.

3 "You shall have no other gods before me.

4 "You shall not make for yourself a carved image, or any likeness of anything that is in heaven above, or that is in the earth beneath, or that is in the water under the earth. 5 You shall not bow down to them or serve them, for I the Lord your God am a jealous God, visiting the iniquity of the fathers on the children to the third and the fourth generation of those who hate me, 6 but showing steadfast love to thousands of those who love me and keep my commandments.

7 "You shall not take the name of the Lord your God in vain, for the Lord will not hold him guiltless who takes his name in vain.

8 "Remember the Sabbath day, to keep it holy. 9 Six days you shall labor, and do all your work, 10 but the seventh day is a Sabbath to the Lord your God. On it you shall not do any work, you, or your son, or your daughter, your male servant, or your female servant, or your livestock, or the sojourner who is within your gates. 11 For in six days the Lord made heaven and earth, the sea, and all that is in them, and rested on the seventh day. Therefore the Lord blessed the Sabbath day and made it holy.

12 "Honor your father and your mother, that your days may be long in the land that the Lord your God is giving you.

13 "You shall not murder.

14 "You shall not commit adultery.

15 "You shall not steal.

16 "You shall not bear false witness against your neighbor.

17 "You shall not covet your neighbor's house; you shall not covet your neighbor's wife, or his male servant, or his female servant, or his ox, or his donkey, or anything that is your neighbor's."

18 Now when all the people saw the thunder and the flashes of lightning and the sound of the trumpet and the mountain smoking, the people were afraid and trembled, and they stood far off 19 and said to Moses, "You speak to us, and we will listen; but do not let God speak to us, lest we die." 20 Moses said to the people, "Do not fear, for God has come to test you, that the fear of him may be before you, that you may not sin." 21 The people stood far off, while Moses drew near to the thick darkness where God was.

1. Who spoke the commandments?

2. Where were the Israelites when they heard these words? Where had they been previously?

3. Why couldn't the people or priests go up the mountain on which God had descended?

PONDER Why were the Israelites given the Ten Commandments?

PRAYER IDEAS Thank God for speaking to you and for saving you from slavery to sin through Jesus Christ just like he saved the Israelites from slavery in Egypt.

Exodus 20:1-3

And God spoke all these words, saying, [2] "I am the LORD your God, who brought you out of the land of Egypt, out of the house of slavery.

[3] "You shall have no other gods before me."

Deuteronomy 6:4-5

"Hear, O Israel: The LORD our God, the LORD is one. [5] You shall love the LORD your God with all your heart and with all your soul and with all your might."

1. What do you think God means when he says that the Israelites are to have "no other gods before me" (Exod 20:3)?

2. According to these passages, what is the most important relationship in life?

3. What false 'gods' compete for people's loyalty today?

PONDER Who is number one in your life?

PRAYER IDEAS Ask God to help you to love him with all your heart, soul and strength. Thank him for Jesus, who remains your faithful saviour even when you are a faithless servant.

Exodus 20:4-6

"You shall not make for yourself a carved image, or any likeness of anything that is in heaven above, or that is in the earth beneath, or that is in the water under the earth. [5] You shall not bow down to them or serve them, for I the LORD your God am a jealous God, visiting the iniquity of the fathers on the children to the third and the fourth generation of those who hate me, [6] but showing steadfast love to thousands of those who love me and keep my commandments."

Exodus 32:1-5

When the people saw that Moses delayed to come down from the mountain, the people gathered themselves together to Aaron and said to him, "Up, make us gods who shall go before us. As for this Moses, the man who brought us up out of the land of Egypt, we do not know what has become of him." [2] So Aaron said to them, "Take off the rings of gold that are in the ears of your wives, your sons, and your daughters, and bring them to me." [3] So all the people took off the rings of gold that were in their ears and brought them to Aaron. [4] And he received the gold from their hand and fashioned it with a graving tool and made a golden calf. And they said, "These are your gods, O Israel, who brought you up out of the land of Egypt!" [5] When Aaron saw this, he built an altar before it. And Aaron made proclamation and said, "Tomorrow shall be a feast to the LORD."

TITUS

ISAIAH 13-27

TEN COMMANDMENTS

1. What things does this command in Exodus 20:4-6 forbid?

3. What are the two consequences of God's 'jealousy' (20:5-6)?

2. Why does God forbid them?

PONDER Does this command rule out the service of false gods, or the false service of the true God? (Hint: Who did the Israelites think they were worshiping in Exodus 32:5?)

PRAYER IDEAS Ask God to help you to serve him the way you ought.

READING 44   EXODUS 20:4-6; JOHN 1:18, 4:19-24, 14:6-10

Exodus 20:4-6

"You shall not make for yourself a carved image, or any likeness of anything that is in heaven above, or that is in the earth beneath, or that is in the water under the earth. 5 You shall not bow down to them or serve them, for I the LORD your God am a jealous God, visiting the iniquity of the fathers on the children to the third and the fourth generation of those who hate me, 6 but showing steadfast love to thousands of those who love me and keep my commandments."

John 1:18

No one has ever seen God; the only God, who is at the Father's side, he has made him known.

John 4:19-24

The woman said to him, "Sir, I perceive that you are a prophet. 20 Our fathers worshiped on this mountain, but you say that in Jerusalem is the place where people ought to worship." 21 Jesus said to her, "Woman, believe me, the hour is coming when neither on this mountain nor in Jerusalem will you worship the Father. 22 You worship what you do not know; we worship what we know, for salvation is from the Jews. 23 But the hour is coming, and is now here, when the true worshipers will worship the Father in spirit and truth, for the Father is seeking such people to worship him. 24 God is spirit, and those who worship him must worship in spirit and truth."

John 14:6-10

Jesus said to him, "I am the way, and the truth, and the life. No one comes to the Father except through me. 7 If you had known me, you would have known my Father also. From now on you do know him and have seen him."

8 Philip said to him, "Lord, show us the Father, and it is enough for us." 9 Jesus said to him, "Have I been with you so long, and you still do not know me, Philip? Whoever has seen me has seen the Father. How can you say, 'Show us the Father'? 10 Do you not believe that I am in the Father and the Father is in me? The words that I say to you I do not speak on my own authority, but the Father who dwells in me does his works."

1. Who is Jesus?

2. If you have 'seen' Jesus, who have you really 'seen'?

PONDER If Christians don't relate to God through the use of visible images or statues, how should you relate to God?

3. What do these passages tell you about the way you are to relate to God today?

PRAYER IDEAS Thank God for revealing himself to you through his Son, Jesus. Ask him to help you to trust in him.

READING 45   EXODUS 20:7; EZEKIEL 20:13-17, 36:16-23

Exodus 20:7

"You shall not take the name of the LORD your God in vain, for the LORD will not hold him guiltless who takes his name in vain."

Ezekiel 20:13-17

"But the house of Israel rebelled against me in the wilderness. They did not walk in my statutes but rejected my rules, by which, if a person does them, he shall live; and my Sabbaths they greatly profaned.

"Then I said I would pour out my wrath upon them in the wilderness, to make a full end of them. [14] But I acted for the sake of my name, that it should not be profaned in the sight of the nations, in whose sight I had brought them out. [15] Moreover, I swore to them in the wilderness that I would not bring them into the land that I had given them, a land flowing with milk and honey, the most glorious of all lands, [16] because they rejected my rules and did not walk in my statutes, and profaned my Sabbaths; for their heart went after their idols. [17] Nevertheless, my eye spared them, and I did not destroy them or make a full end of them in the wilderness."

Ezekiel 36:16-23

The word of the LORD came to me: [17] "Son of man, when the house of Israel lived in their own land, they defiled it by their ways and their deeds. Their ways before me were like the uncleanness of a woman in her menstrual impurity. [18] So I poured out my wrath upon them for the blood that they had shed in the land, for the idols with which they had defiled it. [19] I scattered them among the nations, and they were dispersed through the countries. In accordance with their ways and their deeds I judged them. [20] But when they came to the nations, wherever they came, they profaned my holy name, in that people said of them, 'These are the people of the LORD, and yet they had to go out of his land.' [21] But I had concern for my holy name, which the house of Israel had profaned among the nations to which they came.

[22] "Therefore say to the house of Israel, Thus says the Lord GOD: It is not for your sake, O house of Israel, that I am about to act, but for the sake of my holy name, which you have profaned among the nations to which you came. [23] And I will vindicate the holiness of my great name, which has been profaned among the nations, and which you have profaned among them. And the nations will know that I am the LORD, declares the Lord GOD, when through you I vindicate my holiness before their eyes."

1. What is the significance of God's name? Are names just words?

3. What did God do in response?

2. How did Israel break the third commandment?

PONDER How else could the Lord's name be taken in vain?

PRAYER IDEAS Thank God for being faithful to his promises, even when his people are rebellious. Ask him to help you to obey him.

READING 46   EXODUS 20:7; PHILIPPIANS 2:1-13

Exodus 20:7

"You shall not take the name of the LORD your God in vain, for the LORD will not hold him guiltless who takes his name in vain."

Philippians 2:1-13

So if there is any encouragement in Christ, any comfort from love, any participation in the Spirit, any affection and sympathy, ² complete my joy by being of the same mind, having the same love, being in full accord and of one mind. ³ Do nothing from rivalry or conceit, but in humility count others more significant than yourselves. ⁴ Let each of you look not only to his own interests, but also to the interests of others. ⁵ Have this mind among yourselves, which is yours in Christ Jesus, ⁶ who, though he was in the form of God, did not count equality with God a thing to be grasped, ⁷ but made himself nothing, taking the form of a servant, being born in the likeness of men. ⁸ And being found in human form, he humbled himself by becoming obedient to the point of death, even death on a cross. ⁹ Therefore God has highly exalted him and bestowed on him the name that is above every name, ¹⁰ so that at the name of Jesus every knee should bow, in heaven and on earth and under the earth, ¹¹ and every tongue confess that Jesus Christ is Lord, to the glory of God the Father. ¹² Therefore, my beloved, as you have always obeyed, so now, not only as in my presence but much more in my absence, work out your own salvation with fear and trembling, ¹³ for it is God who works in you, both to will and to work for his good pleasure.

1. At whose name will every knee bow? Who is the Lord?

2. What does this tell you about the importance of this person?

3. How does the third commandment apply to Christians today?

PONDER What practical steps should you take to honour and glorify the name of the Lord in your day-to-day life?

PRAYER IDEAS Ask God to help you to honour his Son so that his name might be glorified.

Exodus 20:8-11

"Remember the Sabbath day, to keep it holy. 9 Six days you shall labor, and do all your work, 10 but the seventh day is a Sabbath to the LORD your God. On it you shall not do any work, you, or your son, or your daughter, your male servant, or your female servant, or your livestock, or the sojourner who is within your gates. 11 For in six days the LORD made heaven and earth, the sea, and all that is in them, and rested on the seventh day. Therefore the LORD blessed the Sabbath day and made it holy."

Deuteronomy 5:12-15

"Observe the Sabbath day, to keep it holy, as the LORD your God commanded you. 13 Six days you shall labor and do all your work, 14 but the seventh day is a Sabbath to the LORD your God. On it you shall not do any work, you or your son or your daughter or your male servant or your female servant, or your ox or your donkey or any of your livestock, or the sojourner who is within your gates, that your male servant and your female servant may rest as well as you. 15 You shall remember that you were a slave in the land of Egypt, and the LORD your God brought you out from there with a mighty hand and an outstretched arm. Therefore the LORD your God commanded you to keep the Sabbath day."

1. What were the Israelites forbidden to do on the Sabbath? Were there any exceptions?

2. To whom does the Sabbath day belong?

3. What reason does God give for this commandment?

PONDER The idea of 'rest' is prominent in the Old Testament. Why do you think this is the case?

PRAYER IDEAS Thank God for creating you. Ask him to help you to remember that you were made for him.

Hebrews 4

Therefore, while the promise of entering his rest still stands, let us fear lest any of you should seem to have failed to reach it. 2 For good news came to us just as to them, but the message they heard did not benefit them, because they were not united by faith with those who listened. 3 For we who have believed enter that rest, as he has said,

"As I swore in my wrath,
'They shall not enter my rest,'"

although his works were finished from the foundation of the world. 4 For he has somewhere spoken of the seventh day in this way: "And God rested on the seventh day from all his works." 5 And again in this passage he said,

TITUS

ISAIAH 13-27

TEN COMMANDMETS

"They shall not enter my rest."

6 Since therefore it remains for some to enter it, and those who formerly received the good news failed to enter because of disobedience, 7 again he appoints a certain day, "Today," saying through David so long afterward, in the words already quoted,

"Today, if you hear his voice,
do not harden your hearts."

8 For if Joshua had given them rest, God would not have spoken of another day later on. 9 So then, there remains a Sabbath rest for the people of God, 10 for whoever has entered God's rest has also rested from his works as God did from his.

11 Let us therefore strive to enter that rest, so that no one may fall by the same sort of disobedience. 12 For the word of God is living and active, sharper than any two-edged sword, piercing to the division of soul and of spirit, of joints and of marrow, and discerning the thoughts and intentions of the heart. 13 And no creature is hidden from his sight, but all are naked and exposed to the eyes of him to whom we must give account. 14 Since then we have a great high priest who has passed through the heavens, Jesus, the Son of God, let us hold fast our confession. 15 For we do not have a high priest who is unable to sympathize with our weaknesses, but one who in every respect has been tempted as we are, yet without sin. 16 Let us then with confidence draw near to the throne of grace, that we may receive mercy and find grace to help in time of need.

Colossians 2:16–18

Therefore let no one pass judgment on you in questions of food and drink, or with regard to a festival or a new moon or a Sabbath. 17 These are a shadow of the things to come, but the substance belongs to Christ. 18 Let no one disqualify you, insisting on asceticism and worship of angels, going on in detail about visions, puffed up without reason by his sensuous mind ...

1. What is the "Sabbath rest" spoken about in Hebrews 4?

2. Who makes it possible for you to enter this 'rest'?

3. What must you avoid or do in order to enter it?

PONDER Does the fourth commandment apply to Christians today? If so, how?

PRAYER IDEAS Thank God for allowing you to enter his rest through the Lord Jesus Christ.

READING 49   EXODUS 20:12; 21:15, 17

Exodus 20:12
"Honor your father and your mother, that your days may be long in the land that the LORD your God is giving you."

Exodus 21:15
"Whoever strikes his father or his mother shall be put to death."

Exodus 21:17

"Whoever curses his father or his mother shall be put to death."

1. What does 'honouring' your parents mean?

2. Is there an age limit on the commandment?

3. What promise is attached to this commandment? Why do you think this is the case?

PONDER What does the fact that we need to put signs on our buses saying, "Please vacate this seat for elderly passengers" tell you about our willingness to obey the fifth commandment?

PRAYER IDEAS Ask God to help you to always honour your father and mother.

READING 50 — MATTHEW 15:1-9, 10:32-39

Matthew 15:1-9

Then Pharisees and scribes came to Jesus from Jerusalem and said, ² "Why do your disciples break the tradition of the elders? For they do not wash their hands when they eat." ³ He answered them, "And why do you break the commandment of God for the sake of your tradition? ⁴ For God commanded, 'Honor your father and your mother,' and, 'Whoever reviles father or mother must surely die.' ⁵ But you say, 'If anyone tells his father or his mother, "What you would have gained from me is given to God," ⁶ he need not honor his father.' So for the sake of your tradition you have made void the word of God. ⁷ You hypocrites! Well did Isaiah prophesy of you, when he said:

⁸ "'This people honors me with their lips,
    but their heart is far from me;
⁹ in vain do they worship me,
    teaching as doctrines the
        commandments of men.'"

Matthew 10:32-39

So everyone who acknowledges me before men, I also will acknowledge before my Father who is in heaven, ³³ but whoever denies me before men, I also will deny before my Father who is in heaven.

³⁴ "Do not think that I have come to bring peace to the earth. I have not come to bring peace, but a sword. ³⁵ For I have come to set a man against his father, and a daughter against her mother, and a daughter-in-law against her mother-in-law. ³⁶ And a person's enemies will be those of his own household. ³⁷ Whoever loves father or mother more than me is not worthy of me, and whoever loves son or daughter more than me is not worthy of me. ³⁸ And whoever does not take his cross and follow me is not worthy of me. ³⁹ Whoever finds his life will lose it, and whoever loses his life for my sake will find it."

1. What point is Jesus making in the Matthew 15 passage?

2. What point is Jesus making in the Matthew 10 passage?

TITUS

ISAIAH 13-27

TEN COMMANDMENTS

PONDER How does Jesus help you to understand how to put the fifth commandment into practice?

PRAYER IDEAS Ask your heavenly Father to help you to love and honour him not only with your lips, but also with your life.

READING 51   EXODUS 20:13; GENESIS 9:6; DEUTERONOMY 20:10-18

Exodus 20:13

"You shall not murder."

Genesis 9:6

"Whoever sheds the blood of man, by man shall his blood be shed, for God made man in his own image."

Deuteronomy 20:10–18

"When you draw near to a city to fight against it, offer terms of peace to it. [11] And if it responds to you peaceably and it opens to you, then all the people who are found in it shall do forced labor for you and shall serve you. [12] But if it makes no peace with you, but makes war against you, then you shall besiege it. [13] And when the LORD your God gives it into your hand, you shall put all its males to the sword, [14] but the women and the little ones, the livestock, and everything else in the city, all its spoil, you shall take as plunder for yourselves. And you shall enjoy the spoil of your enemies, which the LORD your God has given you. [15] Thus you shall do to all the cities that are very far from you, which are not cities of the nations here. [16] But in the cities of these peoples that the LORD your God is giving you for an inheritance, you shall save alive nothing that breathes, [17] but you shall devote them to complete destruction, the Hittites and the Amorites, the Canaanites and the Perizzites, the Hivites and the Jebusites, as the LORD your God has commanded, [18] that they may not teach you to do according to all their abominable practices that they have done for their gods, and so you sin against the LORD your God."

This is the commandment that everyone agrees with and not many people break. But what is it about?

1. Why doesn't the commandment say "You shall not kill"? Why is war sometimes okay? Why is the killing of animals okay?

2. Why is accidentally killing someone not regarded by our courts as murder?

3. Why is deliberately taking a human life wrong?

PONDER Why is society so casual about abortion, while at the same time rejecting capital punishment for murder?

PRAYER IDEAS Ask God to help you to value human life and seek to preserve it.

READING 52   MATTHEW 5:21-26; ROMANS 13:8-10

Matthew 5:21–26

"You have heard that it was said to those of old, 'You shall not murder; and whoever murders will be liable to judgment.' [22] But I say to you that everyone who is angry with his brother will be liable to judgment;

whoever insults his brother will be liable to the council; and whoever says, 'You fool!' will be liable to the hell of fire. 23 So if you are offering your gift at the altar and there remember that your brother has something against you, 24 leave your gift there before the altar and go. First be reconciled to your brother, and then come and offer your gift. 25 Come to terms quickly with your accuser while you are going with him to court, lest your accuser hand you over to the judge, and the judge to the guard, and you be put in prison. 26 Truly, I say to you, you will never get out until you have paid the last penny."

Romans 13:8-10

Owe no one anything, except to love each other, for the one who loves another has fulfilled the law. 9 For the commandments, "You shall not commit adultery, You shall not murder, You shall not steal, You shall not covet," and any other commandment, are summed up in this word: "You shall love your neighbor as yourself." 10 Love does no wrong to a neighbor; therefore love is the fulfilling of the law.

1. What application does Jesus draw from the sixth commandment?

2. How does Paul sum up the commandments (cf. Mark 12:29-31[38])?

3. Is there a difference between breaking a commandment and failing to fulfil it?

PONDER What attitudes and behaviour do you need to do away with in order to fulfil the sixth commandment (e.g. expressions of anger)? What attitudes and behaviour do you need to put into practice?

PRAYER IDEAS Ask God to rescue you from anger and help you to love others the way he has loved you.

READING 53 — EXODUS 20:14, 22:16; GENESIS 1:27-28, 2:18-25

Exodus 20:14

"You shall not commit adultery."

Exodus 22:16

"If a man seduces a virgin who is not betrothed and lies with her, he shall give the bride-price for her and make her his wife."

Genesis 1:27-28

So God created man in his own image, in the image of God he created him; male and female he created them.

28 And God blessed them. And God said to them, "Be fruitful and multiply and fill the earth and subdue it and have dominion over the fish of the sea and over the birds of the heavens and over every living thing that moves on the earth."

Genesis 2:18-25

Then the LORD God said, "It is not good that the man should be alone; I will make him a helper fit for him." 19 Now out of the ground the LORD God had formed every beast of the field and every bird of the heavens and brought them to the man to see what

---

38. Jesus answered, "The most important is, 'Hear, O Israel: The Lord our God, the Lord is one. 30 And you shall love the Lord your God with all your heart and with all your soul and with all your mind and with all your strength.' 31 The second is this: 'You shall love your neighbor as yourself.' There is no other commandment greater than these."

he would call them. And whatever the man called every living creature, that was its name. [20] The man gave names to all livestock and to the birds of the heavens and to every beast of the field. But for Adam there was not found a helper fit for him. [21] So the LORD God caused a deep sleep to fall upon the man, and while he slept took one of his ribs and closed up its place with flesh. [22] And the rib that the LORD God had taken from the man he made into a woman and brought her to the man. [23] Then the man said,

"This at last is bone of my bones
    and flesh of my flesh;
she shall be called Woman,
    because she was taken out of Man."

[24] Therefore a man shall leave his father and his mother and hold fast to his wife, and they shall become one flesh. [25] And the man and his wife were both naked and were not ashamed.

1. Who created sex?

2. What is sex for?

3. Why, then, is sex outside of marriage wrong?

PONDER How does the biblical view of sex differ to society's view?

PRAYER IDEAS Thank God for the gift of sex. Ask him to help you not to wrong others by using your sexuality improperly.

READING 54 1 CORINTHIANS 7:1-5; MATTHEW 5:27-30

1 Corinthians 7:1-5

Now concerning the matters about which you wrote: "It is good for a man not to have sexual relations with a woman." [2] But because of the temptation to sexual immorality, each man should have his own wife and each woman her own husband. [3] The husband should give to his wife her conjugal rights, and likewise the wife to her husband. [4] For the wife does not have authority over her own body, but the husband does. Likewise the husband does not have authority over his own body, but the wife does. [5] Do not deprive one another, except perhaps by agreement for a limited time, that you may devote yourselves to prayer; but then come together again, so that Satan may not tempt you because of your lack of self-control.

Matthew 5:27-30

"You have heard that it was said, 'You shall not commit adultery.' [28] But I say to you that everyone who looks at a woman with lustful intent has already committed adultery with her in his heart. [29] If your right eye causes you to sin, tear it out and throw it away. For it is better that you lose one of your members than that your whole body be thrown into hell. [30] And if your right hand causes you to sin, cut it off and throw it away. For it is better that you lose one of your members than that your whole body go into hell."

1. In 1 Corinthians 7, what does Paul say is the proper context for sex?

2. What attitude should govern the use of your body in marriage?

3. According to Jesus, what evil lies at the heart of adultery?

PONDER What steps do you need to take to ensure that you are pure in the use of your body?

PRAYER IDEAS Ask God to help you to be blameless, ready to be presented to Christ in purity.

READING 55   EXODUS 20:15, 22:1-14

Exodus 20:15
"You shall not steal."

Exodus 22:1-14
If a man steals an ox or a sheep, and kills it or sells it, he shall repay five oxen for an ox, and four sheep for a sheep. 2 If a thief is found breaking in and is struck so that he dies, there shall be no bloodguilt for him, 3 but if the sun has risen on him, there shall be bloodguilt for him. He shall surely pay. If he has nothing, then he shall be sold for his theft. 4 If the stolen beast is found alive in his possession, whether it is an ox or a donkey or a sheep, he shall pay double.

5 "If a man causes a field or vineyard to be grazed over, or lets his beast loose and it feeds in another man's field, he shall make restitution from the best in his own field and in his own vineyard.

6 "If fire breaks out and catches in thorns so that the stacked grain or the standing grain or the field is consumed, he who started the fire shall make full restitution.

7 "If a man gives to his neighbor money or goods to keep safe, and it is stolen from the man's house, then, if the thief is found, he shall pay double. 8 If the thief is not found, the owner of the house shall come near to

God to show whether or not he has put his hand to his neighbor's property. 9 For every breach of trust, whether it is for an ox, for a donkey, for a sheep, for a cloak, or for any kind of lost thing, of which one says, 'This is it,' the case of both parties shall come before God. The one whom God condemns shall pay double to his neighbor.

10 "If a man gives to his neighbor a donkey or an ox or a sheep or any beast to keep safe, and it dies or is injured or is driven away, without anyone seeing it, 11 an oath by the Lord shall be between them both to see whether or not he has put his hand to his neighbor's property. The owner shall accept the oath, and he shall not make restitution. 12 But if it is stolen from him, he shall make restitution to its owner. 13 If it is torn by beasts, let him bring it as evidence. He shall not make restitution for what has been torn.

14 "If a man borrows anything of his neighbor, and it is injured or dies, the owner not being with it, he shall make full restitution."

1. What does the Exodus 22 passage teach you about having respect for the property of others?

2. What motivates stealing?

3. There is more to stealing than just 'breaking and entering'. What are some of the more subtle and sophisticated ways you might be tempted to take what is not yours?

PONDER What steps do you need to take to make sure you don't break the eighth commandment?

PRAYER IDEAS Ask God to help you to be content with what you have. Ask him to help you resist the temptation to take what is not yours.

READING 56   EPHESIANS 4:28; HEBREWS 13:1-5; 1 TIMOTHY 6:17-19

Ephesians 4:28

Let the thief no longer steal, but rather let him labor, doing honest work with his own hands, so that he may have something to share with anyone in need.

Hebrews 13:1-5

Let brotherly love continue. 2 Do not neglect to show hospitality to strangers, for thereby some have entertained angels unawares. 3 Remember those who are in prison, as though in prison with them, and those who are mistreated, since you also are in the body. 4 Let marriage be held in honor among all, and let the marriage bed be undefiled, for God will judge the sexually immoral and adulterous. 5 Keep your life free from love of money, and be content with what you have, for he has said, "I will never leave you nor forsake you."

1 Timothy 6:17-19

As for the rich in this present age, charge them not to be haughty, nor to set their hopes on the uncertainty of riches, but on God, who richly provides us with everything to enjoy. 18 They are to do good, to be rich in good works, to be generous and ready to share, 19 thus storing up treasure for themselves as a good foundation for the future, so that they may take hold of that which is truly life.

1. What should the thief do? Why?

2. How can you keep your life free from the love of money?

3. How should you use your money and possessions?

PONDER How can you cultivate contentment with what you have? How can you become more generous?

PRAYER IDEAS Ask God to help you to be rich in good works and generosity.

Exodus 20:16

"You shall not bear false witness against your neighbor."

Deuteronomy 19:15-21

"A single witness shall not suffice against a person for any crime or for any wrong in connection with any offense that he has committed. Only on the evidence of two witnesses or of three witnesses shall a charge be established. 16 If a malicious witness arises to accuse a person of wrongdoing, 17 then both parties to the dispute shall appear before the LORD, before the priests and the judges who are in office in those days. 18 The judges shall inquire diligently, and if the witness is a false witness and has accused his brother falsely, 19 then you shall do to him as he had meant to do to his brother. So you shall purge the evil from your midst. 20 And the rest shall hear and fear, and shall never again commit any such evil among you. 21 Your eye shall not pity. It shall be life for life, eye for eye, tooth for tooth, hand for hand, foot for foot."

1. *What do these passages tell you about what God thinks of lying?*

2. *What attitude lies behind the testimony of a false witness?*

3. *Is there anyone who never lies, slanders or gossips?*

PONDER The Devil is the "father of lies" (John 8:44**[39]**). What impact do lies have on your relationship with God?

PRAYER IDEAS Ask God to help you to trust him always, rejecting all lies and falsehood.

Matthew 12:33-37

"Either make the tree good and its fruit good, or make the tree bad and its fruit bad, for the tree is known by its fruit. 34 You brood of vipers! How can you speak good, when you are evil? For out of the abundance of the heart the mouth speaks. 35 The good person out of his good treasure brings forth good, and the evil person out of his evil treasure brings forth evil. 36 I tell you, on the day of judgment people will give account for every careless word they speak, 37 for by your words you will be justified, and by your words you will be condemned."

Ephesians 4:15-16

Rather, speaking the truth in love, we are to grow up in every way into him who is the head, into Christ, 16 from whom the whole body, joined and held together by every joint with which it is equipped, when each part is working properly, makes the body grow so

---

39. "You are of your father the devil, and your will is to do your father's desires. He was a murderer from the beginning, and has nothing to do with the truth, because there is no truth in him. When he lies, he speaks out of his own character, for he is a liar and the father of lies."

TITUS

ISAIAH 13-27

TEN COMMANDMETS

that it builds itself up in love.

Ephesians 4:25–32

Therefore, having put away falsehood, let each one of you speak the truth with his neighbor, for we are members one of another. ²⁶ Be angry and do not sin; do not let the sun go down on your anger, ²⁷ and give no opportunity to the devil. ²⁸ Let the thief no longer steal, but rather let him labor, doing honest work with his own hands, so that he may have something to share with anyone in need. ²⁹ Let no corrupting talk come out of your mouths, but only such as is good for building up, as fits the occasion, that it may give grace to those who hear. ³⁰ And do not grieve the Holy Spirit of God, by whom you were sealed for the day of redemption. ³¹ Let all bitterness and wrath and anger and clamor and slander be put away from you, along with all malice. ³² Be kind to one another, tenderhearted, forgiving one another, as God in Christ forgave you.

1. Why is speech so important? What does it show about the speaker?

2. What sort of speech should you do away with?

3. What should you speak? How should you speak?

PONDER What should be the purpose or goal of all your speech? How does this contrast with the attitude that lies behind lying, gossip and slander?

PRAYER IDEAS Ask God to help you to always speak the truth in love.

READING 59　　　　　　EXODUS 20:17; ECCLESIASTES 4:4, 5:10-11 ☐

Exodus 20:17

"You shall not covet your neighbor's house; you shall not covet your neighbor's wife, or his male servant, or his female servant, or his ox, or his donkey, or anything that is your neighbor's."

Ecclesiastes 4:4

Then I saw that all toil and all skill in work come from a man's envy of his neighbor. This also is vanity and a striving after wind.

Ecclesiastes 5:10-11

He who loves money will not be satisfied with money, nor he who loves wealth with his income; this also is vanity. ¹¹ When goods increase, they increase who eat them,

and what advantage has their owner but to see them with his eyes?

1. How does this commandment relate to the previous four (Exod 20:13-16 ⁴⁰)?

2. What do these passages have to say about the attitudes that lie behind the desire for money or possessions?

---

40. "You shall not murder.
¹⁴ "You shall not commit adultery.

¹⁵ "You shall not steal.
¹⁶ "You shall not bear false witness against your neighbor."

3. Why is the one who loves money never satisfied by the very thing he loves?

PONDER How are these passages a wake-up-call to those who live in materialistic societies driven by envy?

PRAYER IDEAS Ask God to help you to be content with what you have. Also ask him to help you not to get hung up about what you don't have.

READING 60   1 TIMOTHY 6:9-10, 17; EPHESIANS 5:5; MARK 8:36 ☐

1 Timothy 6:9-10

But those who desire to be rich fall into temptation, into a snare, into many senseless and harmful desires that plunge people into ruin and destruction. ¹⁰ For the love of money is a root of all kinds of evils. It is through this craving that some have wandered away from the faith and pierced themselves with many pangs.

1 Timothy 6:17

As for the rich in this present age, charge them not to be haughty, nor to set their hopes on the uncertainty of riches, but on God, who richly provides us with everything to enjoy.

Ephesians 5:5

For you may be sure of this, that everyone who is sexually immoral or impure, or who is covetous (that is, an idolater), has no inheritance in the kingdom of Christ and God.

Mark 8:36

For what does it profit a man to gain the whole world and forfeit his soul?

1. What temptations and traps exist for those who love money?

2. Why is greed idolatry?

3. Why is the love of money and riches so serious?

PONDER What is the path to contentment?

PRAYER IDEAS Ask God to help you to put your hope in him and in him alone.

APPENDIX

ADDITIONAL PASSAGES REFERRED TO ...

2 Kings 18-20 (Reading 21)

In the third year of Hoshea son of Elah, king of Israel, Hezekiah the son of Ahaz, king of Judah, began to reign. 2 He was twenty-five years old when he began to reign, and he reigned twenty-nine years in Jerusalem. His mother's name was Abi the daughter of Zechariah. 3 And he did what was right in the eyes of the LORD, according to all that David his father had done. 4 He removed the high places and broke the pillars and cut down the Asherah. And he broke in pieces the bronze serpent that Moses had made, for until those days the people of Israel had made offerings to it (it was called Nehushtan). 5 He trusted in the LORD, the God of Israel, so that there was none like him among all the kings of Judah after him, nor among those who were before him. 6 For he held fast to the LORD. He did not depart from following him, but kept the commandments that the LORD commanded Moses. 7 And the LORD was with him; wherever he went out, he prospered. He rebelled against the king of Assyria and would not serve him. 8 He struck down the Philistines as far as Gaza and its territory, from watchtower to fortified city.

9 In the fourth year of King Hezekiah, which was the seventh year of Hoshea son of Elah, king of Israel, Shalmaneser king of Assyria came up against Samaria and besieged it, 10 and at the end of three years he took it. In the sixth year of Hezekiah, which was the ninth year of Hoshea king of Israel, Samaria was taken. 11 The king of Assyria carried the Israelites away to Assyria and put them in Halah, and on the Habor, the river of Gozan, and in the cities of the Medes, 12 because they did not obey the voice of the LORD their God but transgressed his covenant, even all that Moses the servant of the LORD commanded. They neither listened nor obeyed.

13 In the fourteenth year of King Hezekiah, Sennacherib king of Assyria came up against all the fortified cities of Judah and took them. 14 And Hezekiah king of Judah sent to the king of Assyria at Lachish, saying, "I have done wrong; withdraw from me. Whatever you impose on me I will bear." And the king of Assyria required of Hezekiah king of Judah three hundred talents of silver and thirty talents of gold. 15 And Hezekiah gave him all the silver that was found in the house of the LORD and in the treasuries of the king's house. 16 At that time Hezekiah stripped the gold from the doors of the temple of the LORD and from the doorposts that Hezekiah king of Judah had overlaid and gave it to the king of Assyria. 17 And the king of Assyria sent the Tartan, the Rab-saris, and the Rabshakeh with a great army from Lachish to King Hezekiah at Jerusalem. And they went up and came to Jerusalem. When they arrived, they came and stood by the conduit of the upper pool, which is on the highway to the Washer's Field. 18 And when they called for the king, there came out to them Eliakim the son of Hilkiah, who was over the household, and Shebnah the secretary, and Joah the son of Asaph, the recorder.

19 And the Rabshakeh said to them, "Say to Hezekiah, 'Thus says the great king, the king of Assyria: On what do you rest this trust of yours? 20 Do you think that mere words are

strategy and power for war? In whom do you now trust, that you have rebelled against me? 21 Behold, you are trusting now in Egypt, that broken reed of a staff, which will pierce the hand of any man who leans on it. Such is Pharaoh king of Egypt to all who trust in him. 22 But if you say to me, "We trust in the LORD our God," is it not he whose high places and altars Hezekiah has removed, saying to Judah and to Jerusalem, "You shall worship before this altar in Jerusalem"? 23 Come now, make a wager with my master the king of Assyria: I will give you two thousand horses, if you are able on your part to set riders on them. 24 How then can you repulse a single captain among the least of my master's servants, when you trust in Egypt for chariots and for horsemen? 25 Moreover, is it without the LORD that I have come up against this place to destroy it? The LORD said to me, Go up against this land, and destroy it."

26 Then Eliakim the son of Hilkiah, and Shebnah, and Joah, said to the Rabshakeh, "Please speak to your servants in Aramaic, for we understand it. Do not speak to us in the language of Judah within the hearing of the people who are on the wall." 27 But the Rabshakeh said to them, "Has my master sent me to speak these words to your master and to you, and not to the men sitting on the wall, who are doomed with you to eat their own dung and to drink their own urine?"

28 Then the Rabshakeh stood and called out in a loud voice in the language of Judah: "Hear the word of the great king, the king of Assyria! 29 Thus says the king: 'Do not let Hezekiah deceive you, for he will not be able to deliver you out of my hand. 30 Do not let Hezekiah make you trust in the LORD by saying, The LORD will surely deliver us, and this city will not be given into the hand of the king of Assyria.' 31 Do not listen to Hezekiah, for thus says the king of Assyria: 'Make your peace with me and come out to me. Then each one of you will eat of his own vine, and each one of his own fig tree, and each one of you will

drink the water of his own cistern, 32 until I come and take you away to a land like your own land, a land of grain and wine, a land of bread and vineyards, a land of olive trees and honey, that you may live, and not die. And do not listen to Hezekiah when he misleads you by saying, The LORD will deliver us. 33 Has any of the gods of the nations ever delivered his land out of the hand of the king of Assyria? 34 Where are the gods of Hamath and Arpad? Where are the gods of Sepharvaim, Hena, and Ivvah? Have they delivered Samaria out of my hand? 35 Who among all the gods of the lands have delivered their lands out of my hand, that the LORD should deliver Jerusalem out of my hand?'"

36 But the people were silent and answered him not a word, for the king's command was, "Do not answer him." 37 Then Eliakim the son of Hilkiah, who was over the household, and Shebna the secretary, and Joah the son of Asaph, the recorder, came to Hezekiah with their clothes torn and told him the words of the Rabshakeh.

19:1 As soon as King Hezekiah heard it, he tore his clothes and covered himself with sackcloth and went into the house of the LORD. 2 And he sent Eliakim, who was over the household, and Shebna the secretary, and the senior priests, covered with sackcloth, to the prophet Isaiah the son of Amoz. 3 They said to him, "Thus says Hezekiah, This day is a day of distress, of rebuke, and of disgrace; children have come to the point of birth, and there is no strength to bring them forth. 4 It may be that the LORD your God heard all the words of the Rabshakeh, whom his master the king of Assyria has sent to mock the living God, and will rebuke the words that the LORD your God has heard; therefore lift up your prayer for the remnant that is left." 5 When the servants of King Hezekiah came to Isaiah, 6 Isaiah said to them, "Say to your master, 'Thus says the LORD: Do not be afraid because of the words that you have heard, with which the servants of the king of Assyria have reviled me.

7 Behold, I will put a spirit in him, so that he shall hear a rumor and return to his own land, and I will make him fall by the sword in his own land.'"

8 The Rabshakeh returned, and found the king of Assyria fighting against Libnah, for he heard that the king had left Lachish. 9 Now the king heard concerning Tirhakah king of Cush, "Behold, he has set out to fight against you." So he sent messengers again to Hezekiah, saying, 10 "Thus shall you speak to Hezekiah king of Judah: 'Do not let your God in whom you trust deceive you by promising that Jerusalem will not be given into the hand of the king of Assyria. 11 Behold, you have heard what the kings of Assyria have done to all lands, devoting them to destruction. And shall you be delivered? 12 Have the gods of the nations delivered them, the nations that my fathers destroyed, Gozan, Haran, Rezeph, and the people of Eden who were in Telassar? 13 Where is the king of Hamath, the king of Arpad, the king of the city of Sepharvaim, the king of Hena, or the king of Ivvah?'"

14 Hezekiah received the letter from the hand of the messengers and read it; and Hezekiah went up to the house of the LORD and spread it before the LORD. 15 And Hezekiah prayed before the LORD and said: "O LORD, the God of Israel, enthroned above the cherubim, you are the God, you alone, of all the kingdoms of the earth; you have made heaven and earth. 16 Incline your ear, O LORD, and hear; open your eyes, O LORD, and see; and hear the words of Sennacherib, which he has sent to mock the living God. 17 Truly, O LORD, the kings of Assyria have laid waste the nations and their lands 18 and have cast their gods into the fire, for they were not gods, but the work of men's hands, wood and stone. Therefore they were destroyed. 19 So now, O LORD our God, save us, please, from his hand, that all the kingdoms of the earth may know that you, O LORD, are God alone."

20 Then Isaiah the son of Amoz sent to Hezekiah, saying, "Thus says the LORD, the God of Israel: Your prayer to me about Sennacherib king of Assyria I have heard. 21 This is the word that the LORD has spoken concerning him:

"She despises you, she scorns you—
    the virgin daughter of Zion;
she wags her head behind you—
    the daughter of Jerusalem.

22 "Whom have you mocked and reviled?
    Against whom have you raised your
        voice
and lifted your eyes to the heights?
    Against the Holy One of Israel!
23 By your messengers you have mocked the
        Lord,
    and you have said, 'With my many
        chariots
I have gone up the heights of the
        mountains,
    to the far recesses of Lebanon;
I felled its tallest cedars,
    its choicest cypresses;
I entered its farthest lodging place,
    its most fruitful forest.
24 I dug wells
    and drank foreign waters,
and I dried up with the sole of my foot
    all the streams of Egypt.'

25 "Have you not heard
    that I determined it long ago?
I planned from days of old
    what now I bring to pass,
that you should turn fortified cities
    into heaps of ruins,
26 while their inhabitants, shorn of strength,
    are dismayed and confounded,
and have become like plants of the field
    and like tender grass,
like grass on the housetops,
    blighted before it is grown.

27 "But I know your sitting down
    and your going out and coming in,

and your raging against me.
28 Because you have raged against me
and your complacency has come into
my ears,
I will put my hook in your nose
and my bit in your mouth,
and I will turn you back on the way
by which you came.

29 "And this shall be the sign for you: this year eat what grows of itself, and in the second year what springs of the same. Then in the third year sow and reap and plant vineyards, and eat their fruit. 30 And the surviving remnant of the house of Judah shall again take root downward and bear fruit upward. 31 For out of Jerusalem shall go a remnant, and out of Mount Zion a band of survivors. The zeal of the LORD will do this.

32 "Therefore thus says the LORD concerning the king of Assyria: He shall not come into this city or shoot an arrow there, or come before it with a shield or cast up a siege mound against it. 33 By the way that he came, by the same he shall return, and he shall not come into this city, declares the LORD. 34 For I will defend this city to save it, for my own sake and for the sake of my servant David."

35 And that night the angel of the LORD went out and struck down 185,000 in the camp of the Assyrians. And when people arose early in the morning, behold, these were all dead bodies. 36 Then Sennacherib king of Assyria departed and went home and lived at Nineveh. 37 And as he was worshiping in the house of Nisroch his god, Adrammelech and Sharezer, his sons, struck him down with the sword and escaped into the land of Ararat. And Esarhaddon his son reigned in his place.

20:1 In those days Hezekiah became sick and was at the point of death. And Isaiah the prophet the son of Amoz came to him and said to him, "Thus says the LORD, 'Set your house in order, for you shall die; you shall not recover.'" 2 Then Hezekiah turned his face to the wall and prayed to the LORD, saying,

3 "Now, O LORD, please remember how I have walked before you in faithfulness and with a whole heart, and have done what is good in your sight." And Hezekiah wept bitterly. 4 And before Isaiah had gone out of the middle court, the word of the LORD came to him: 5 "Turn back, and say to Hezekiah the leader of my people, Thus says the LORD, the God of David your father: I have heard your prayer; I have seen your tears. Behold, I will heal you. On the third day you shall go up to the house of the LORD, 6 and I will add fifteen years to your life. I will deliver you and this city out of the hand of the king of Assyria, and I will defend this city for my own sake and for my servant David's sake." 7 And Isaiah said, "Bring a cake of figs. And let them take and lay it on the boil, that he may recover."

8 And Hezekiah said to Isaiah, "What shall be the sign that the LORD will heal me, and that I shall go up to the house of the LORD on the third day?" 9 And Isaiah said, "This shall be the sign to you from the LORD, that the LORD will do the thing that he has promised: shall the shadow go forward ten steps, or go back ten steps?" 10 And Hezekiah answered, "It is an easy thing for the shadow to lengthen ten steps. Rather let the shadow go back ten steps." 11 And Isaiah the prophet called to the LORD, and he brought the shadow back ten steps, by which it had gone down on the steps of Ahaz.

12 At that time Merodach-baladan the son of Baladan, king of Babylon, sent envoys with letters and a present to Hezekiah, for he heard that Hezekiah had been sick. 13 And Hezekiah welcomed them, and he showed them all his treasure house, the silver, the gold, the spices, the precious oil, his armory, all that was found in his storehouses. There was nothing in his house or in all his realm that Hezekiah did not show them. 14 Then Isaiah the prophet came to King Hezekiah, and said to him, "What did these men say? And from where did they come to you?" And Hezekiah said, "They have come from a far country, from Babylon." 15 He

said, "What have they seen in your house?" And Hezekiah answered, "They have seen all that is in my house; there is nothing in my storehouses that I did not show them."

16 Then Isaiah said to Hezekiah, "Hear the word of the LORD: 17 Behold, the days are coming, when all that is in your house, and that which your fathers have stored up till this day, shall be carried to Babylon. Nothing shall be left, says the LORD. 18 And some of your own sons, who shall be born to you, shall be taken away, and they shall be eunuchs in the palace of the king of Babylon." 19 Then said Hezekiah to Isaiah, "The word of the LORD that you have spoken is good." For he thought, "Why not, if there will be peace and security in my days?"

20 The rest of the deeds of Hezekiah and all his might and how he made the pool and the conduit and brought water into the city, are they not written in the Book of the Chronicles of the Kings of Judah? 21 And Hezekiah slept with his fathers, and Manasseh his son reigned in his place.

2 Kings 16:1–16 (Reading 24)

In the seventeenth year of Pekah the son of Remaliah, Ahaz the son of Jotham, king of Judah, began to reign. 2 Ahaz was twenty years old when he began to reign, and he reigned sixteen years in Jerusalem. And he did not do what was right in the eyes of the LORD his God, as his father David had done, 3 but he walked in the way of the kings of Israel. He even burned his son as an offering, according to the despicable practices of the nations whom the LORD drove out before the people of Israel. 4 And he sacrificed and made offerings on the high places and on the hills and under every green tree.

5 Then Rezin king of Syria and Pekah the son of Remaliah, king of Israel, came up to wage war on Jerusalem, and they besieged Ahaz but could not conquer him. 6 At that time Rezin the king of Syria recovered Elath for Syria and drove the men of Judah from Elath, and the Edomites came to Elath, where they dwell to this day. 7 So Ahaz sent messengers to Tiglath-pileser king of Assyria, saying, "I am your servant and your son. Come up and rescue me from the hand of the king of Syria and from the hand of the king of Israel, who are attacking me." 8 Ahaz also took the silver and gold that was found in the house of the LORD and in the treasures of the king's house and sent a present to the king of Assyria. 9 And the king of Assyria listened to him. The king of Assyria marched up against Damascus and took it, carrying its people captive to Kir, and he killed Rezin.

10 When King Ahaz went to Damascus to meet Tiglath-pileser king of Assyria, he saw the altar that was at Damascus. And King Ahaz sent to Uriah the priest a model of the altar, and its pattern, exact in all its details. 11 And Uriah the priest built the altar; in accordance with all that King Ahaz had sent from Damascus, so Uriah the priest made it, before King Ahaz arrived from Damascus. 12 And when the king came from Damascus, the king viewed the altar. Then the king drew near to the altar and went up on it 13 and burned his burnt offering and his grain offering and poured his drink offering and threw the blood of his peace offerings on the altar. 14 And the bronze altar that was before the LORD he removed from the front of the house, from the place between his altar and the house of the LORD, and put it on the north side of his altar. 15 And King Ahaz commanded Uriah the priest, saying, "On the great altar burn the morning burnt offering and the evening grain offering and the king's burnt offering and his grain offering, with the burnt offering of all the people of the land, and their grain offering and their drink offering. And throw on it all the blood of the burnt offering and all the blood of the sacrifice, but the bronze altar shall be for me to inquire by." 16 Uriah the priest did all this, as King Ahaz commanded.

Isaiah 5:1-7 (Reading 39)

Let me sing for my beloved
my love song concerning his vineyard:
My beloved had a vineyard
on a very fertile hill.
2 He dug it and cleared it of stones,
and planted it with choice vines;
he built a watchtower in the midst of it,
and hewed out a wine vat in it;
and he looked for it to yield grapes,
but it yielded wild grapes.

3 And now, O inhabitants of Jerusalem
and men of Judah,
judge between me and my vineyard.
4 What more was there to do for my
vineyard,
that I have not done in it?
When I looked for it to yield grapes,
why did it yield wild grapes?

5 And now I will tell you
what I will do to my vineyard.
I will remove its hedge,
and it shall be devoured;
I will break down its wall,
and it shall be trampled down.
6 I will make it a waste;
it shall not be pruned or hoed,
and briers and thorns shall grow up;
I will also command the clouds
that they rain no rain upon it.

7 For the vineyard of the LORD of hosts
is the house of Israel,
and the men of Judah
are his pleasant planting;
and he looked for justice,
but behold, bloodshed;
for righteousness,
but behold, an outcry!

Feedback on this resource

We really appreciate getting feedback about our resources—not just
suggestions for how to improve them, but also positive feedback and
ways they can be used. We especially love to hear that the resources
may have helped someone in their Christian growth.

You can send feedback to us via the 'Feedback' menu in our online
store, or write to us at PO Box 225, Kingsford NSW 2032, Australia.

matthiasmedia

Matthias Media is an evangelical publishing ministry that seeks to persuade all Christians of the Bible-shaped, theological truth of God's purposes in Jesus Christ, and equip them with high-quality resources, so that they will:

- abandon their lives to the honour and service of Christ in daily holiness and decision-making
- pray constantly in Christ's name for the growth of his gospel
- speak the Bible's life-changing word whenever and however they can—in the home, in the world and in the fellowship of his people.

It was in 1988 that we first started pursuing this mission, and in God's kindness we now have more than 300 different ministry resources being used all over the world. These resources range from Bible studies and books through to training courses and audio sermons.

To find out more about our large range of very useful resources, and to access samples and free downloads, visit our website:

www.matthiasmedia.com.au

How to buy our resources

1. Direct from us over the internet:
   - in the US: www.matthiasmedia.com
   - in Australia and the rest of the world: www.matthiasmedia.com.au

> Register at our website for our **free** regular email update to receive information about the latest new resources, **exclusive special offers**, and free articles to help you grow in your Christian life and ministry.

2. Direct from us by phone:
   - in the US: 1 866 407 4530
   - in Australia: 1800 814 360 (Sydney: 9663 1478)
   - international: +61-2-9663-1478

3. Through a range of outlets in various parts of the world. Visit **www.matthiasmedia.com.au/international.php** for details about recommended retailers in your part of the world, including www.thegoodbook.co.uk in the United Kingdom.

4. Trade enquiries can be addressed to:
   - in the US and Canada: sales@matthiasmedia.com
   - in Australia and the rest of the world: sales@matthiasmedia.com.au

THE ESV BIBLE

Since its much-anticipated release in late 2001, the English Standard Version (ESV) Bible has won increasing acceptance in churches throughout the US, England and Australia as an accurate, readable Bible for general use.

The secret of the ESV's success has been its ability to balance two crucial factors in Bible translation. On the one hand, it seeks to be an 'essentially literal' translation, retaining some of the form and flavour of the ancient text, and sticking as closely as possible to its thought-forms and imagery. At the same time, the ESV strives to be flowing and readable for a modern audience.

This balancing act is never possible to achieve perfectly, but the ESV is thought by many to do the best job of any English translation currently available.

This makes it suitable for a wide variety of purposes, including public reading and preaching, private and small group study, memorization, and so on.

"The English Standard Version is noticeably better than the current most popular English translations of the Bible. The ESV brings us closer to what the authors actually wrote, and therefore what the Author actually says. Bible readers, teachers and preachers: this is the translation we have been waiting for, contemporary but more precisely accurate."

Rev. Dr John Woodhouse
Principal, Moore College, Sydney

To find out more about the ESV, and to view online samples, go to

www.matthiasmedia.com.au/ESV